On Transforming Africa
Discourse with Africa's Leaders

Kofi Buenor Hadjor

Jointly Published by:

Africa World Press, Inc.
P.O. Box 1892
Trenton, New Jersey 08607
(609) 695-3766

THIRD WORLD
COMMUNICATIONS
Kwame Nkrumah House 173 Old Street
London EC1V 9NJ United Kingdom

DEDICATION

I dedicate this book to the memory of
Kwame Nkrumah,
Africa's great son,
who bequeathed to the continent
an agenda for her socio-economic liberation
and to the youth of Africa
upon whose shoulders rests the major responsibility
for implementing the Nkrumaist agenda
to build Africa anew.

Each generation must, out of relative obscurity, discover its mission, fulfill it, or betray it.

—Frantz Fanon

Adinkra Symbol (Asante)

EPA (Handcuff)

"Onii a n'epa da wo nsa no, ne akowa ne wo."

"You are the slave of him whose handcuffs you wear."

ACKNOWLEDGEMENTS

I wish to thank
Laura and Ruth Brako, Yvonne Cowan,
Priti Dave, Jonathan Lorie, Ruby Ofori,
Zagba Oyortey and Richard Renwick,
my colleagues at Third World Communications,
for the various roles they each played
while I worked on this book.

My thanks also go to
Dede-Esi Amanor and Jacquiline King for proofreading,
Peter Clarke for designing the cover,
Neze Onyeama for long hours of discussion on *Discourse,*
Patrick Smith for some editorial involvement,
Karen Lawrence for typing the manuscript,
and Pauline Tiffen and Gregg Wright for the index.

On the personal level I wish to express
my special thanks to
Mike Awuah-Asamoah and Justina Donkor
and their children, the Blays, Dan Owusu-Afari,
and Dr. Franklin Moustafa of Korlebu Hospital
for the humanity they showed me in 1982.

And finally, my thoughts go to
Olu and Gwen, Tanya and Shirley,
Brooke, Patrick, Amanda Mensah,
Santhoshni Perera, Yaa Frempomaa,
Claude and Reggie, Marie Ologbosere
and the many friends
who have shared so much with me
over long and short periods.

Africa World Press, Inc.
P.O. Box 1892
Trenton, N.J. 08607

Third World Communications
Kwame Nkrumah House
173 Old Street, London
EC1V 9NJ U.K.

First Published in 1987

Typeset by TypeHouse of Pennington

Library of Congress Catalog Card Number: 86-73049

Book trade orders for edition published by
1: Third World Communications, Kwame Nkrumah House,
   173 Old Street, London EC1V 9NJ, U.K.
2: Africa World Press, P.O. Box 1892, Trenton,
   New Jersey 08607, U.S.A.

British Library Cataloguing in Publication Data
Hadjor, Kofi Buenor, 1939-
   On Transforming Africa
   Includes index
ISBN: (US Edition): 0-86543-044-6 (Cloth)
                    0-86543-045-4 (Paper)
ISBN: (UK Edition): 1-87010-100-6 (Cloth)
                    1-87010-105-7 (Paper)

Cover design by Peter Clark

CONTENTS

PREFACE

The writing of this book began in late Summer 1985 and was completed in late Autumn of the same year. In the intervening period events have unfolded in Africa at a rather dramatic pace. We have not felt it necessary to update this book since recent events merely confirm the analysis outlined in the text. The debate that has blown up over sanctions in South Africa and the snubbing of African leaders by Britain and the United States is only the culmination of a process of interaction evident during the past two or so decades. Although we have left the text as it is we have added a chapter on the special United Nations Assembly discussion on Africa, as an Afterword. We felt that this special Assembly throws further light on the acute leadership problems facing Africa.

We have included a glossary to help the reader understand the intent behind some of the key words used in this book. Many of the terms deployed in this text do not follow established convention. We have used words selectively and in a partisan way, with a view to emphasizing the potential for change. Often, certain terms acquire a specific nuance because of our political direction. Thus, for example, Africa is not used as a geographical but a political entity. Africa has been used in an undifferentiated way in order to stress the common social and political problems facing the continent.

As the title, *On Transforming Africa: Discourse With Africa's Leaders*, is rather long, I would like this book to be referred to simply as *Discourse*, if I had my way.

I am not unaware of the fact that there is a movement in the correct direction of rewriting English vocabulary, so that words such as "chairman" and "mankind" lose their male connotations. I apologize for deliberately maintaining the conventional terminology. This is done not out of disregard for the women's movement, since I agree that the old terms are chauvinist. It is done primarily because no viable standard alternative has yet been established. Should that happen, and this book see a second issue, I hope to set the record straight. In the meantime I would reassure all my readers that I am with them in the struggle for a non-chauvinist vocabulary.

Kofi Buenor Hadjor
London, September 1986

FOREWORD

One of the great tragedies in Africa is that too often well-placed proponents of mass-oriented change fail to share their useful experiences with mass-oriented activists.

History helps only those who learn its lessons well. There is no telling how many mistakes in the struggle for economic progress and social justice could have been averted had the correct lessons from history been learned within the context of the experiences of people who were well positioned in history.

Kofi Buenor Hadjor, a press aide to Kwame Nkrumah, began to gather some experiences that would nurture his understanding of the national leadership question in Africa. In writing his essay, *Discourse With Africa's Leaders*, Hadjor becomes one of the relatively few well-positioned Africans to share his experiences with those who would want to see Africa transformed and characterized by economic progress and social justice.

Hadjor's essay is a critique of the African condition and of those responsible for the present state of affairs. Written at a relentless pace, it is a work of impatience and exudes a determination to get to the heart of the matter. Hadjor does not waste the reader's time as he takes us on a compelling voyage to a world of exploitation, underdevelopment and repression that is uniquely African.

Hadjor's essay represents an important contribution to the

understanding of the African socio-economic and political malaise. At the risk of simplification, it can be argued that political literature in Africa is either *reflective* or *reactive*. Many African writers have written interesting essays which reflect the emerging state of affairs. Such writings contain intellectual insight but because of their distance from life have the flavor of academia and little direct consequence. Other articles are more immediate and direct as they represent a reaction to specific events such as changes in government or an outburst of political conflict.

Although such efforts appear to have direct relevance, they are essentially reactions rather than the work of conscious, deliberate and comprehensive thought. One of the merits of Hadjor's work is that it is both reflective and reactive. It reflects on the relevance of the past for the present and hardly loses sight of the urgent issues of the moment. In this sense, *Discourse* follows and develops the political tradition established by Fanon and Cabral.

Hadjor's essay is serving notice from the masses to those who carry on oblivious to the scale of the problems facing Africa. Everyone with an interest in Africa is aware of its profound problems, but fear prevents many from openly discussing them. Hadjor articulates many of the sentiments and fears that we only like to half admit. Nevertheless, Hadjor's work is not pessimistic. Nor, it should be stated, is it a work of naive hope.

For Hadjor, the economic, political and social tensions tearing Africa apart are not the outcome of destiny and its immutable laws. He recognizes the difficulties facing Africa in the aftermath of the colonial period but argues that the failure to confront them was, above all, a failure of political leadership. The failures of African politics are many, but errors can be rectified. Hadjor's message is that just as

Africa's problems were constructed by humans, so they are open to human solutions. He offers a strong antidote to those who, to all intents and purposes, have given up on Africa. Hadjor rescues Africa from those who see it as the inevitable object of international charity and puts forward a case for treating it as a subject susceptible to political solutions.

Hadjor's essay takes the form of a discourse with Africa's leaders. It is written as a critique of that leadership and seeks to challenge the fundamental assumptions behind political debate. Hadjor is not simply interested in providing answers, he wants Africa's leaders to re-examine their position—the very basis of their authority and legitimacy. Hadjor puts forward the case for a new type of leader—one that emerges through interaction with society, through struggle in the interest of the oppressed masses.

For the author, African leaders and indeed politics in general have an existence that is external to the lives of the vast majority in society. The implication of Hadjor's argument is that until African leaders work concretely in the interest of the African masses—even with the best intentions—they will remain obstacles to African economic progress and social justice.

Although the essay takes the form of a discourse with Africa's leaders, it is clear that Hadjor's real target is the new generation of Africans. *The emphasis in this book is on African youth learning from the mistakes of their elders.* This is not surprising since the author is desperately concerned that Africa's tradition of liberation and transformative vision should not be lost to the younger generations. To those who were active and influential during the unfolding of this drama, it is perhaps a reminder of a tradition that too many of us have forgotten.

For Africans, especially those involved in public affairs

like myself, this is not a book to be treated lightly. There will be some who will try to laugh it off as the sentimental reminder of political innocence. Others, especially those with influence in government, will react with rage, disclaim all responsibility and denounce it as the work of a presumptuous agitator. It would be a shame if such a response were to insulate concerned Africans from examining this book. For at the very least, we owe it to ourselves to account for the past and state clearly whether our original objectives were unrealistic or whether we subsequently lost our way.

In hindsight, it is clear that had African governments pursued proposals suggested in the essay, many of the continent's difficulties could have been avoided. Of course, hindsight has the advantage of distance. There is little purpose in wishing things had been otherwise. What is done is done and we must concentrate the mind on the future, but learning correctly the lessons of the past.

At one time or another many of us in government were drawn towards transformative social and economic policies advocated in the essay. Some of us were also quite ready to act on such policies. However, those voices favoring colonial structures prevailed. A few, a very few stood up and fought, but for most it was easier to compromise and adapt to the dominant mood in government.

The conventional wisdom that prevailed in the cabinet offices of Africa was that the business of government was to govern and not to change and transform. Such advice made perfect sense to civil servants used to bureaucratic routine. It also made sense for governments whose commitment to power gradually became self-perpetuating and governing became an end in itself. Those Africans interested in transformation were either thrown aside or turned into window-dressing critics. In the end, governing became a euphemism for technical administration and politicians adopted the language and mannerisms of superior civil servants. In most places inertia and complacency exhausted the vocabulary of politics, while the masses suffered and were robbed of their rights to participation in decision-making.

Discourse marks the beginning of a critical stage in African politics. Its publication comes at an appropriate stage of Africa's development. The old politics of the post-colonial era are reaching a dead end. It is essential that failure in the past should not provoke a fear of new experiments. Fortunately, there are signs that experiments are again taking place. A rebirth of Africa's liberation tradition is evident in the struggle to liberate South Africa and Namibia. This struggle may yet spark off a wider search for new solutions and new ideas. All over the nation-states of Africa, oppressed masses are finding more and better ways of organizing against exploitation and repression and for the building of democratic institutions.

Hadjor is right to insist that the time for a new course has arrived, for the time has already been appointed by the masses who now see that it is "not yet uhuru" in the post-colonial era.

It is a pleasure to introduce the reader to this exciting contribution to African political discourse. I am confident that the author's aim of promoting a reassessment of African national leadership will strike a chord among all concerned Africans.

Togba-Nah Tipoteh*

*Togba-Nah Tipoteh is Economics Research Professor at the Institute of Social Studies in the Hague. He was Economic Planning Minister in Liberia.

I

An Open Letter To Concerned Africans

It requires no great leap in imagination to understand that Africa's extreme problems require—dare I say— extreme solutions. There are times in history when change becomes imperative and nothing less than a revolution in attitudes will suffice. Such a time is now. The reconstruction of a new African leadership is set on the agenda of history.

Not so long ago Africans looked to the future with hope and confidence. The burning desire for change which swept the continent led to a flowering of new ideas and eventually forced the old colonial masters to make their exit. For those of us who were young and active during this era, it seemed as if it was only a matter of time before Africa assumed its rightful place in the world order. History, however, never gives guarantees. And today many of our earlier dreams are dismissed as hopelessly naive and unrealistic. With Africa in disarray such cynicism is quite understandable. But isn't there the danger of reading history backwards and finding in the past only justifications for the failures of today?

It is much easier to accommodate the present-day realities than to recapture the motivation and ideals of the movement for change that set Africa alight. Nevertheless, we had every right to expect major strides forward once independence had been won. It is necessary to emphasize this point in the most forceful terms. It is essential to reiterate this conjunction because with every new *coup*, and every new famine, the mood of demoralization and fatalism strengthens its grip over the African consciousness. Worse still, Africa's activists and thinkers have grown too old too fast. With every setback the reluctance to face our problems gathers in strength. There is now the danger that even our cherished tradition of discussion and debate will be lost. Too many dictators around! What we have written is addressed to those Africans who have not yet lost all hope and are prepared to stand up and reverse the existing trends.

Let's begin in the middle of things. During the years 1964–66, I served my apprenticeship as a press aide in the Publicity Secretariat of the late President Kwame Nkrumah. As a relatively minor figure in the government and of the younger generation we were left pretty much to our own devices. We got on with the job but knew very little about what Ghana's senior leaders were thinking about the problems of the day. Looking back on the past, the military coup that overthrew Nkrumah should not have come as a surprise. The overwhelming impression one has of the period is one of exhilaration combined with the underlying sense that something was going wrong. From the vantage point of today everything is much clearer. The government was getting out of touch. The movement behind Nkrumah had become detached. The only active force was the old African colonial establishment.

Two months after the coup, in exile in Conakry, I had my first serious discussion with Nkrumah. The initial reaction of Nkrumah to the overthrow of his regime was to find an explanation for his demise in the realm of *realpolitik*. During one of our discussions he handed me a copy of Machiavelli's *The Prince* and suggested that had he but followed the author's advice on political ruthlessness the military coup could have been averted. It is very much to Nkrumah's credit, as his post-1966 writings show, that he was soon able to go beyond this first impression and develop a far-reaching analysis of the African political scene.

As I write, I have a vivid recollection of one such meeting. It was, I think, in August 1967 at a sunset hour and we sat in the open air of his residence, Villa Syli. Present on this particular occasion were Ambrose Yankey Jr. and Leonard Blay, his most trusted security boys. Hardly had we finished the business at hand when Nkrumah handed me a copy of Fitch and Oppenheimer's book *Ghana: End of An Illusion*, asking if I had read it. "Yes," I replied, "it's an excellent analysis." He furiously scolded me for liking a book that was rather unkind to him. "This is a book of amateur Marxists who watched me and my Ghana from outside," he complained.

"You African journalists," he shouted, "must tell the world who I actually am—a convinced Marxist socialist."

As it happens, I did read Machiavelli and anything else that I could lay my hands on which would explain what went wrong. It was in Conakry that I first read Fanon, especially his *Wretched of the Earth* which my exile companion, John K. Tettegah, now Ghana's Ambassador to the Soviet Union, gave me as a present. It did not take me long to realize that Fanon's analysis had much more to offer than Machiavelli and many of the other classics. Tettegah and I literally devoured the chapter on "The Pitfalls of National Consciousness" as we felt its analysis was too true to the Ghanaian situation.

During this period, too, I had a very rare opportunity of

meeting Africa's exemplary leader, Amilcar Cabral, who, until he was assassinated on January 20, 1973 by the Portuguese, had his *Partido Africano da Independencia da Guine e Capo Verde* (PAIGC) office in Conakry. Listening to Cabral's informal lectures and analyses of the African situation convinced me that in terms of ideological clarity, he was far ahead of his fellow leaders of the day.

Tettegah and I were first introduced to Cabral by Victor Maria and Gill Fernandez sometime in late 1967 during a flight between Cairo and Conakry. "Ghana has entered the phase of the class struggle," I remember Cabral's first words to us; "whether it will be violent or otherwise, I don't know," he added.

Victor Maria and Gill Fernandez were PAIGC's representatives in Cairo in the late sixties. The former became his country's first foreign minister and later prime minister before his downfall in 1983. Gill Fernandez is now Guinea-Bissau's Ambassador at the United Nations.

My spell in Guinea coupled with my two-year career with the Cairo-based Afro-Asian People's Solidarity Organization (AAPSO) where Nkrumah had sent me to represent his out-of-power Convention People's Party helped to provide the foundations of my world outlook.

Although we did not know it, the setback in Ghana was to set the pattern for the rest of Africa. By the end of the sixties, the die was cast. The seventies saw the disintegration of the continent and the destruction of its political life. During the eighties political instability has been compounded by economic disaster and now Africa is paying the price in human misery. After these events it was difficult for anyone to retain his naivete. Observing developments firsthand in Guinea, Tanzania, Kenya, Egypt and Algeria, I have been struck by the essentially common character of our problems. Despite regional and cultural variations, the same curse seems to afflict us all.

With Africa on the verge of an historic disaster silence would be criminal. This essay is written as a direct challenge to Africa's leadership. We are not interested in recrimination. The lessons of our past experiences must be assimilated but not to simply point the finger—rather to avoid recurrent mistakes. Above all, we are concerned with the new generation of activists and thinkers—those who will lead Africa tomorrow. However, Africa needs all of its people. As Nkrumah showed through the developments in his ideas, no one is too old to learn and change their ways. Anyone in a position of influence has a duty to at least confront the questions raised by the experience of the past three decades.

Independence has seemed to make little difference to Africa. Too often Africans have allowed others to give them independence instead of realizing it themselves. A fear of change descended very early on Africa. Instead of *transformation*, the key motto of Africa's leaders was *conservation*. A change of personnel without a change of institutions was insufficient to ensure Africans that independence would truly be theirs.

Without its own institutions Africa has lost the ability to control its affairs. No other part of the world is more dependent on external forces than Africa. The decisions that influence African lives are not made in Accra, Nairobi or Addis Ababa. They are made in London, Paris, Washington or Moscow. No part of the world can remain isolated and self-sufficient. In Africa, however, external influence has become power itself. It is not at all unusual for many African governments to be more reliant on the backing they receive from abroad than on the support of their own people.

The failure to confront the problem of change explains

Africa's subsequent collapse. As history showed so many times before it is not possible to stay still—if Africa did not go forward it had to fall behind. And fall behind it did. With every year that passed Africa proved less capable of realizing even the most elementary aspirations of its people. Internal convulsion and discord has produced a protracted period of instability which has now gone beyond two decades.

In the meantime, Africa's institutions which were designed to regulate its subjection in the colonial era continued to ensure its subservience in the world order. *Absolutely* nothing had changed. Instead, as the old institutions became less and less able to cope, Africa's *relative* position declined. The refusal to come to terms with the problem of change necessarily led to *regression*. As a result, the issue is no longer about the merits of change but of survival.

Our economic and political institutions stand discredited. Yet, Africa's leaders are fervently opposed to new alternatives. Every suggestion which implies the radical transformation of Africa is dismissed as unrealistic. This fear of the unknown leads to the grotesque conclusion that sees the realism of famine, of permanent political instability and economic decline as history's destiny for Africa.

It requires no great leap in imagination to understand that Africa's extreme problems require—dare I say—extreme solutions. The clock cannot be turned back. Tinkering with the economy will not make the famine or the debt crisis go away. Regional rivalries, civil wars and military coups cannot be legislated out of existence. Nor can we depend on a resurgence of Western interest and charity to help Africa on its feet again.

Africa's leaders can no longer shirk their responsibility. They must either lead or make way for those who are not prepared to evade the tasks facing them. There are times in history when change becomes imperative and nothing less than a revolution in attitudes will suffice. Such a time is now.

The reconstruction of a new African leadership is set on the agenda of history. But we cannot turn back the clock either. Inspiration and important lessons can be gained from the ideas of Africa's great leaders. The tradition of Nkrumah, Fanon, Lumumba and Cabral has withstood the test of time. If this tradition is to mean anything it will not do to simply repeat it—it has to be further developed in line with the pressing problems of the day.

To face Africa as it is and not as we would like to see it is to begin to find a solution. Solutions will not come out of our heads. It requires the collective efforts of all concerned Africans. That's why the emergence of a new Africa cannot be an act of individual courage, fortitude and example. Of course such characteristics are much needed for the resolution of our crisis. But real leadership means activating Africa's people. It is only through mass mobilization of opinion that the will and determination to see things through can be established. To reawaken the continent is to begin to give back to its people mastery over their future.

Until now Africa's leaders have looked at the problems, declared that they are difficult and drawn the conclusion that therefore they were impossible to solve. Our new leaders will be different, they will see the difficulties but will argue "yes, there are no easy solutions. All the more reason to fight harder. All the more reason to involve everyone." It is this difference in attitude that can sow the seeds of a revolution in Africa's life.

What we offer our readers is a perspective on confronting the African condition. It is the product of observation, experience and discussion with friends and comrades over many years. We have not minced our words or spared feelings or sentiment to attempt to come to terms with the outstanding issues of the day.

As a perspective for change, we think this essay will contribute towards clarifying what needs to be done. At the same time we don't see it as a prescription for Africa's solution. We say this not out of false modesty but from the recognition that the solution to Africa's difficulties does not lie in words but in action.

If this essay provokes others to write and debate then the stage will have been set for a constructive engagement of African political thought. Such clarification and debate could be the first step towards the testing of ideas through organization and action. Lastly, at the risk of yielding to sentimentality, we dedicate this work to Kwame Nkrumah. Were he still to be around today, we are convinced that he would have fully shared our concern and many of our thoughts.

II

On The Leadership Crisis in Africa

The crisis of African leadership will not be resolved through discovering better individual leaders. Its decline cannot be reduced to individual weakness. It is the product of the separation of the leaders from the masses. To reverse this process requires not so much new individual leaders but a new relationship between leaders and the mass movement.... That is why the building of a political movement is a precondition for the exercise of leadership.

The tanks roll in and take up their positions on the deserted streets of Kampala announcing the demise of another African political regime.* Few mourn the departure of the deposed leader and fewer expect much from the self-proclaimed saviours of the country. It has happened many times before—not only in Uganda but throughout the continent. Every coup and every change of government provokes less enthusiasm than the time before.

A few countries have avoided the upheavals of major power struggles and coups. Leaders of these countries have had a good run for their money. But "stability" at what price?

*This scene refers to General Tito Okello's coup against Milton Obote's regime.

Their "stability" depends on outwitting potential opponents, anticipating protests and pre-empting upheavals. Both military leaders and civilian politicians rely not only on popular support, but on the demobilization of the masses.

What about the revolutionary regimes of Africa? From Guinea-Bissau to Mozambique the dreams have been replaced by a gray pragmatism that only evokes indifference, apathy and even hostility. The ideology may be different but for ordinary people the experience of life is the same as in the rest of Africa.

Cynics, and there are not a few, claim that all this is inevitable. They dismiss the hopes and aspirations of Fanon, Lumumba and Cabral as the ineffectual ravings of dreamers and, pointing to the stability of Banda's Malawi or Kenyatta's Kenya, declare that only *realpolitik* works. Are they right? Must Africa be doomed to a cycle of unrepresentative and unpopular regimes, out of touch with the people they purport to lead?

The decline of authority

It is easy to forget that not so long ago Africa had a fine tradition of popular leadership. During the fifties and sixties the anti-colonial struggle threw up a generation of popular leaders with strong roots among the masses. Kwame Nkrumah, Sekou Toure, Julius Nyerere and others did not have to fix elections or rely on the army as a substitute for popular support. Mobilizing millions of Africans they single-mindedly pursued the struggle for political independence.

Observers called many of the anti-colonial leaders *charismatic*—men with exceptional powers or qualities. Perhaps they were exceptional. What gave Nkrumah or Sekou Toure so much authority, however, was not their personal brilliance, but an ability to personify the need and dreams of the masses. The yearning for freedom, dignity and a better way of life acquired a voice through those at the helm of the anti-colonial movement. Their strength was not simply their own but derived from the strength of the popular feeling for change. From this interaction between leader and led sprang genuine political authority. Of course, it did not happen automatically for genuine authority has to be earned, but once earned, the political leader could enjoy the support and goodwill of those who endowed him with authority.

We have come a long way from the past when authority was *earned* to today when authority is simply *declared* by a self-styled leader. What a change in the very definition of leadership! Contrast an Amilcar Cabral who could articulate the broad sentiments of ordinary people with the majority of African leaders who can articulate only their self-interest.

Today, the lack of genuine political authority highlights the estrangement of the African political elite from their societies. Whatever the difference in style of ruling, African leaders share a common mistrust of the people they claim to represent. Authority here is based on a monopoly over the instruments of coercion and control over a significant portion of society's resources.

Here is a typical scene. A swift coup and the former soldier is installed in the presidential palace. He promises freedom, prosperity and a new way of life. Since nothing changes, the brief upsurge of hope is followed by a protracted period of despondency. To stay in the saddle, he unleashes a reign of force—so-called troublemakers and opposition politicians are jailed, exiled or banned from political activity. Without a shred of authority he is forced to establish a semblance of legitimacy for his rule. He calls for an election. Parties are banned and politicians are detained during the pre-election campaign and on it goes.

The failure of political leadership in Africa is all too evident. It would be tempting to blame this failure on the particular leader concerned. Greed and other individual failures have no doubt played a part. However, we are not discussing individual failures here and there but a clear pattern of political impasse that appears to affect the whole continent. An obsession with the trappings of power is manifest in the case of a General Amin. Yet not every African leader can be indicted for selfishness or for a lust for power. The overthrow of Nkrumah and the slow progress of Tanzania under Nyerere show that despite a commitment to total transformation, the problem of leadership remains unresolved. Let's look at the roots of this problem.

Leaders and led

It was the experience of the anti-colonial struggle that influenced the complexion of African leadership for decades to come. In every colonial struggle the imperialist powers try to separate the leaders from the masses. The French and British colonial authorities developed an art of flattering or buying off their most prominent opponents. Presidents Banda, Kenyatta, Houphouet-Boigny and Leopold Senghor are proof of the success of this strategy. Often, however, this strategy doesn't work. In that case, the colonial authorities crack down on the mass movement, detain and isolate its grassroots activists and, through this method, hope to isolate those at the top. When even this option failed, the colonial authorities simply murdered the national leaders—Lumumba, Cabral—hoping that their successors would be more susceptible to manipulation.

The objective of this colonial strategy is based on the assumption that it is easier to deal with a group of isolated leaders than a volatile mass movement. As individuals, cut off from mass pressure, leaders are more inclined to compromise and collaborate. From the imperialist point of view it is easier to make concessions to an individual leader's desire for status and power than it is to meet the demands of the mass movement for real change. It is possible to see this dynamic unfolding before our eyes today in South Africa. The ruthless racist regime combines a strategy of terror against local activists with an offer of an olive branch to those *responsible* black politicians who are prepared to negotiate. The aim of the exercise is to turn African leaders into negotiating partners.

In general, the transfer of power was successful, from a colonial point of view, precisely because the negotiating partners were to some extent immunized from mass pressure. Hence political independence often represented a compromise with the past colonial institutions. Most important of all, by the time negotiations were completed many African leaders were more dependent on the colonial institutions than on mass support.

Negotiations did not succeed in every situation. Radical movements in Guinea-Bissau, Angola and Mozambique succeeded in wresting power from their colonial masters. Sekou Toure in Guinea refused to compromise with the French authorities. But even in these cases the colonial strategy of separating leaders from the mass movement had some considerable effect.

Where the colonialists did not succeed in creating a conflict of interest between leaders and led they managed to weaken the links between grassroots activists and the prominent nationalists. This was effected through the application of coercion and through the exacerbation of ethnic differences and rivalries. The civil war that is at present ravaging Angola is testimony to the devastating impact of the colonial strategy.

It is important to emphasize the colonial legacy because, although it does not exhaust the problem, it throws light on the obstacles to the exercise of effective leadership in post-colonial Africa. There is yet another problem. In every African nation the new leadership had a fundamental choice. Would it rely on the energy of its mass support or would it look to the existing state institutions for the exercise of its authority? For the moderates the choice was clear from the outset—the masses were unpredictable while the civil service or the army were there to serve. More radical leaders like Nkrumah and Nyerere were aware of the "professional dangers of power" and yet they could not see how they could make do without the old institutions. In practice, most African governments attempted to combine governing through the old colonial institutions with a degree of political mobilization.

Before long, however, the new leaders became either willing or unwilling prisoners of the state administration. It was easier to follow the tried and tested methods of the past than to innovate new popular institutions. The civil service was well trained and educated in administration and in the exercise of power and the anti-colonial movement was not. A ready-made, all-purpose institution with a worked out routine and clear procedures seemed a preferable alternative to the unknown. As a result, African leaders became more and more reliant on the state machinery and political innovation simply consisted of setting up one public enterprise after another.

The fusion of the newly independent government with the old state bureaucracy had an overwhelming impact on political relations. Those in power were drawn towards administrative rather than political solutions. Even those leaders who were aware of the need for mass support found themselves choosing the expediency of administrative convenience over the harder task of winning political support from the people. The very nature of leadership changed fundamentally. Instead of articulating the aspirations of the masses, African heads of government began to speak the language of bureaucrats and administrators.

The dependence of African leaders on the institutions of the state was necessarily at the expense of popular participation. Indeed, bureaucratic procedure and administration represents the very antithesis of mass involvement. Even radical administrations in Ghana and Guinea fell under the spell of the state bureaucracy. As the political command lost touch with its grassroots supporters the role of state institutions became more important. Slowly, at first almost imperceptibly, the attitude of the leaders began to change. Whereas before the mass movement was seen as the source of authority, it increasingly began to be defined as the problem.

A few leaders like Nkrumah tried to stay in touch with the aspirations of ordinary people. But because he became trapped inside the state administration and distant from the grassroots, the army and the civil service had no problem getting rid of him. Other leaders had no inhibitions about lining up with the state administration against the remnants of the mass movement.

Before too long after independence the newly forged relationship between the political command and state administrators began to manifest its elitist predilections. Throughout the continent the new leaders became accomplices to the exclusion of the masses from politics. They did not need mass movements but political institutions that were accountable only to them. Repression and political control got rid of hotheads and, once the mass movement was demobilized, African governments could set about defining the meaning of political participation.

The African leader, dependent above all on the state, looked upon political activism only with suspicion. He needed political institutions, not to activate, but to control. This is the secret behind the emergence of a one-party system. Where a one-party system could not be implemented, elections were fixed or postponed, ensuring the longevity of the government.

The exclusion of the masses from politics and the general clampdown on political activism led to a growing concentration of power. This explains the emergence of the omnipotent president who holds the reins of power in his own hands. Ironically, on closer inspection the all-powerful leader turns out to be not so powerful. Power through usurpation is also power without legitimacy. Without mass support the leader requires the cooperation of the bureaucracy and the army. In reality his influence is constrained by the lack of independent support. Real power resides with the state machine. The leader rules with the permission of those who run this machine. That is why so many of those in authority, who yesterday seemed all-powerful, now reside in exile pondering what went wrong.

While leaders come and go the old colonial institutions have survived and continue to administer African societies. Even relatively popular leaders who have managed to remain in office, like Julius Nyerere, find that they can do little without the cooperation of the civil service. At the end of the day it is the vested interests of the state administrators that decides whether a particular policy is implemented or ignored. Without mass support even the most charismatic political personalities remain ineffective against the opposition of the civil service and the army.

The tragic decline of African leadership is synonymous with its bureaucratization. Leadership that relies not on mobilization, but on the curbing of mass involvement, necessarily rules by declaration or force. The exclusion of the people from political participation breeds passivity and cynicism. Under these circumstances political life is replaced by administrative convenience. The African head of state ceases to be the voice of the masses and becomes the frontman for the state. This pattern is so well entrenched that even the newly established popular coup-maker gravitates towards negotiations with army and civil service personnel rather than establishing a popular base of support.

The crisis of leadership

The crisis of African leadership will not be resolved through discovering better individual leaders. Its decline cannot be reduced to individual weakness. It is the product of the separation of the leaders from the masses. To reverse this process requires not so much new individual leaders, as the Nigerian literary figure, Chinua Achebe, would make us believe, but a new relationship between leaders and the mass movement.

The most important lesson of the past decades can be learned from the experience of those leaders like Nkrumah, Sekou Toure and Nyerere who have tried to change society for the better but have failed. This failure was *inevitable* given their emphasis on personal authority and adaptation to the existing institutions of the state. All three would have liked mass support for their policies. But such support does not arise spontaneously. It has to be fought for and, above all, it has to be organized!

For the new African leader, leadership cannot mean adapting to the old colonial structures. Real leadership means organizing the masses and establishing new institutions through which the sentiments of the people can be expressed.

Leaders without followers are like the emperor without any clothes, as Emperor Bokassa discovered. A popular following has to be earned through being held accountable. That is why the building of a political movement is a precondition for the exercise of leadership. The involvement of activists and the participation of the masses is essential for the new African leader. Without such participation leadership is never tested, it is only assumed. Indeed, it is only through the interaction between the leader and the political movement that real authority can be acquired and maintained.

It was the lack of organization that allowed the energy of the anti-colonial movement to be dissipated. Without strong organization the separation of leaders from the masses became inevitable. This is the starting point for the present crisis of political leadership in Africa. Every concerned African who is determined to rectify this problem must address the experience of the past two decades. Leadership through the barrel of a gun or leadership through mobilizing people to take control over their lives! These are the alternatives that will decide the destiny of Africa in the decade ahead.

III

On The Party For Change

For if you think that you can manage a country without letting the people interfere, if you think the people upset the game by their mere presence, whether they slow it down or whether by their mere ignorance they sabotage it, then you must have no hesitation: you must keep the people out. Now, it so happens that when the people are invited to partake in the management of the country, they do not slow the movement down but on the contrary they speed it up.

In an underdeveloped country, the party ought to be organized in such a fashion that it is not simply content with having contacts with the masses. The party is not an administration responsible for transmitting government orders. It is the energetic spokeman and incorruptible defender of the masses.

—Franz Fanon

A handful of politicians run Africa. Family ties and business connections provide a network for political discussion and conflict. Everyone else is excluded from political life. Indeed, politics is frowned upon as not the business of ordinary people.

Looking back on the past two or three decades, every serious African politician must be acutely aware of the problem of organization. The nationalist parties of yesterday have turned into paper organizations run by bureaucrats and careerists. Mass movements have turned into empty shells. This destruction of organized political energy provides the most striking indictment of African leadership. It shows that African leaders survive solely through the destruction of political life. More than anything, the paralysis of active political life exposes their lack of authority.

As we argued in the preceding chapter, the building of a political movement is a precondition for the exercise of leadership. Without organization there can be no leadership in the real sense of the term—just a collection of individuals sounding off and making appeals. It is only through organization that a relationship is established between those who represent and those whose aspirations are represented.

Organization activates political creativity and provides a framework for commitment and involvement. This framework for involvement is something that no leader can do without. Those who are involved also acquire the sentiment of responsibility for the objectives of their organization. In contrast, non-involvement breeds only passivity and indifference. Political support means very little in the absence of involvement. It only becomes an active force if it is organized. That is why the exercise of authority is so clearly intertwined with the question of organization.

Ideas and political objectives only acquire meaning through organization. It is only when activists set about organizing that their ideas can be tested. Those ideas that do not prove resilient to organization are ones that have no relevance in everyday life. However, ideas that stimulate organization acquire greater immediacy as more and more people begin to coalesce around them. Organization shapes ideas in their practical detail and provides a framework through which objectives acquire life.

We can see this in relation to Africa's past. The yearning for freedom and independence always existed in a latent form in the colonial era. But it took the arrival of the nationalist movement to give this yearning some practical meaning. Through organization the idea of freedom was transformed into a tangible possibility which could attract mass support.

Learning from past mistakes

African leaders have always shown a talent for making fine declarations and far-reaching promises. However, the real test of political leadership is to be found in the sphere of organization. Speeches can enthuse but they remain mere opinions unless acted upon. It is only through organization that political ideas acquire reality. The best criterion for assessing African leadership is not its ideology or program but its organization. An organization such as the Kenya African National Union (KANU), which is exclusively directed towards elections, immediately indicates that it is not in the business of educating, mobilizing or transforming society. Organization cannot lie. Through organization political purpose acquires a concrete meaning.

Nationalist leaders became so concerned with restricting opposition that their entire intellectual energies went towards developing justifications for a one-party regime. Julius Nyerere wrote at length about the irrelevance of the Westminster parliamentary model for Africa. According to Nyerere, African democracy was not inconsistent with a one-party system. Nyerere argued against those who would object: "to minds molded by Western parliamentary traditions and Western concepts of democratic institutions, the idea of an organized opposition group has become so familiar that its absence immediately raises a cry of 'dictatorship'. " Praising the virtues of the one-party system became the common anthem of African nationalist leaders.

As it happens the one-party system is not necessarily inferior to a multi-party one. However, the frantic obsession with the issue indicates that the nationalist leadership had lost sight of the anti-colonial movement's dreams. The task facing this leadership was not the elimination of opposition but the transformation of society. Governing is not itself an end but a means to one. Unfortunately, the post-colonial organization became directed towards the maintenance of governmental power rather than the realization of social change. The radical impetus behind the mass movement somehow got lost and organization ceased to activate; its sole concern now was to *conserve*. The nationalist party now became an organization of the *status quo*. This meant that leaders like Nyerere and Nkrumah could no longer give their radical ideas an organizational expression. Without political mobilization and the coherent organization of grassroots pressure the foundation for the pursuit of a radical program does not exist. Without institutions that promote activism and political mobilization it is not possible to sustain radical nationalism as a viable strategy at the level of government. The one-party system easily breeds a false sense of security. It often confuses the absence of organized opposition with popular support.

The main achievement of organization in the one-party system in Africa is the depoliticization of the masses. The problem of mass depoliticization is an endemic one throughout Africa. Parties with different national characteristics and political programs have all failed to come to grips with the problem of maintaining popular support.

It is customary to differentiate between African nationalist parties according to their program, ideology and organizational structure. Observers often distinguish between mass and elite parties or those with conservative or radical ideologies. It is clear that an elitist party like the Kenya African National Union (KANU) has little in common with a mass radical movement like the *Partido Africano da Independencia da Guine e Capo Verde* (PAIGC) of Guinea Bissau. Yet closer inspection reveals that often African nationalist parties with conflicting aims and ideologies end up undistinguishable as far as their practice is concerned. Often it is only rhetoric that differentiates radical parties from their conservative cousins.

National variations notwithstanding, radical socialist parties such as Ghana's Convention People's Party (CPP), Guinea's *Parti Democratique de Guinea* (PDG), Tanzania's Tanzania African National Union (TANU) and later *Chama Cha Mapinduzi* (CCM) have all shown a disturbing tendency towards organizational sclerosis. At the outset all three parties demonstrated considerable skill in mobilizing popular support. During the early phase of party building there existed an active relationship between organization and the masses. This heroic period (in Ghana 1949-51, Guinea 1954-56, Tanzania 1958-61) saw the flourishing of organizational innovation and mass participation. This was the era when party activities went beyond episodic electioneering.

However, once the radical parties established their national dominance, politics in the narrow sense of the term became the norm. The parties still retained a formal framework for participation and still advocated radical objectives—but internal life was changing under the growing influence of professional politicians. In these circumstances the ideology, program and organization of the CPP, PDG or CCM became irrelevant. What counted now was the exercise of power rather than the mobilization of the masses.

Attempts by individual leaders like Kwame Nkrumah or

Nyerere to give their party a radical direction was doomed to failure. A party of career politicians was no longer susceptible to grassroots pressure—indeed it actively avoided it. Moreover, as parties of government, the CPP, PDG, and CCM were parties of administration closely allied to the bureaucracy. An informal alliance of political careerists and civil servants ran party affairs and ordinary members were excluded from all meaningful participation. To reverse this trend required *political* solutions; unfortunately Nkrumah, Sekou Toure and Nyerere looked to *organizational* ones. Time and again the parties were reorganized and each time with less and less of an effect.

In 1959, in a major speech commemorating the Tenth Anniversary of the CPP, Nkrumah demanded the reorganization of the party to ensure a continuity with the movement's original principles. Important organizational changes were implemented including the establishment of a youth wing and other auxiliary bodies. Yet nothing changed. Nkrumah returned to this theme of organizational renewal on numerous occasions. In his famous "Dawn" speech of May 1961, Nkrumah was forced to attack the corruption and selfishness of party officials and announced his intention to take control over the direction of the party. Again the CPP was reorganized. Sadly, Nkrumah, like other radical leaders, soon discovered that changing organizational structures is insufficient to stimulate the renewal of political activism and commitment. That requires transformation and not reorganization. All along the problem was not so much organization but the social composition of the organization. A party of careerists can be nothing but a party of careerists no matter how many times it is reorganized.

The demise of the nationalist party as a living force is intimately connected to its social composition. Even in their heyday the nationalist parties were dominated by the urbanized, educated and relatively prosperous sections of African societies. The teachers, civil servants and other professionals of the colonial period became the politicians of the nationalist movement and of the post-colonial era. With the arrival of independence these groups were able to translate influence over the nationalist party into political power. As a social stratum this group of political leaders were primarily interested in acquiring access to resources rather than social change. This interest was directly reflected in the orientation of the governing party. Through its monopoly over political influence mass organizations were redirected towards the narrow concerns of the new African elite.

Since nationalist parties fell into the hands of a small but influential elite their role as a force for mobilization became marginal. They became the exclusive preserve of professional politicians. It is at this point that the African nationalist party ceases to be a movement and becomes a machine. To be sure, African leaders wanted their machine to be active and popular. But devoid of any active relationship with the day to day problems of society, political parties fell into decline, attracting the interest of only a handful of careerists. Thus the parties became too exclusive to make a significant political impact. At the same time the nationalist parties were not exclusive enough. Of their members they asked nothing more than episodic electoral support. The step of entering the ranks of the party had no political significance. It was merely an administrative transaction—an exchange of money for the party card. Membership bestowed no special privileges or responsibilities. Members who only enjoyed the dubious right to be led existed in a one-way relationship with their leaders. Fairly soon political life disintegrated and political leaders became generals without armies.

The main lesson of past experience is that a political movement cannot be sustained without the active participation of party members. And it cannot play the role of a movement if it becomes the exclusive preserve of professional politicians.

A party of activists

The question that needs to be answered is: how can a party involve its supporters and maintain a high level of activity without falling into the trap of being too exclusive?

The strength of a political movement depends on its political activists. Political activists ensure that the party remains in touch with the grassroots. Every party of change needs to be a party of activists. Party activists, of course, promote party doctrine into the language of everyday life. But they have to do more than that. They are the ears of the party. Listening to the concerns of ordinary people, they have to sensitize the party to the mood and passion of the masses—teaching and learning at the same time.

Political activists are not born—they have to be trained. The existing parties of Africa are characterized by the passivity of their supporters. In fact, everything is designed to exclude supporters from direct political involvement.

The new party of change represents the opposite approach. Its survival depends on creating the conditions for participation and a high level of activism. If the party is to demand the commitment of its members it must set about educating and training them. Members do not have to become political giants but they have to become familiar with the principles of the party and committed to fighting for it.

A politically educated membership is an effective force for promoting change. Through their action they can inspire others with a sense of purpose and extend the influence of the party. Equally important is the simple fact that an educated membership is the best guarantee of a healthy political life inside the party. Trained members are not likely to become yes-men. They will insist that problems are clarified and changes in tactics and new policies are properly justified to the new membership. Activists, who themselves are accustomed to the habit of leadership, can ensure that their own leaders are properly accountable to the party.

A party of change has to be a party of activists because only those who are directly involved will want to make the party their own. A party that belongs to its activists is also one where the party leader himself is directly dependent on the party members. This conception directly contradicts political life in Africa today, where parties are owned lock, stock and barrel by those at the top.

Only petty careerists and insecure leaders need worry about a party of activists. There is nothing more educative for a leader than grassroots pressure. The insights and criticisms of activists are essential for forcing individual leaders to face difficult problems and to remind them of their tasks. An energetic membership brings into the party those experiences of everyday existence which the leadership can ignore only at their peril. It is the relationship between political activists and their leaders that transforms vague ideas and general principles into precise policies for action. If this is carried out then the party becomes a university of leadership and authority. With such a party no leader need stand alone. The strength that derives from an organization of trained political activists allows African leaders to make the hard decisions that inevitably arise in the process of transforming Africa.

Organization and the people

A party of political activists is by definition an exclusive one, although its exclusiveness is not based on the promotion of special or sectional interests. It has to be such because only an organization of trained individuals can generate the dynamism necessary to change social life. A party that accepts or actually desires nothing from its members is an organization that has little ambition to change the world. In such an organization the passivity of the membership accurately reflects the acceptance by the party of life as it is.

It is often claimed that an organization of activists is an elitist one. This misses the fundamental point. To equate activism with passivity is to eradicate the distinction between transforming and accepting the African condition. Every new idea is initially the property of a minority. Only a fool would suggest that this minority postpones fighting for its ideas until everyone else has caught up and agreed with it. Such an approach benefits only those who are attached to present-day society and directly benefit from it.

Although an organization of political activists has a distinct existence it cannot be separate from the masses. This is not a matter of choice but of political necessity. The whole purpose of the party is to organize and activate people. No one will support a party that is distant from their concerns. Ordinary people will only identify with a party that is responsive to everyday problems and needs. And a party can only lead if it has assimilated the concerns and hopes of its supporters into its policies and programs. Unless people feel that it is *their* party, suspicion and the fear of manipulation will prevent the exercise of political dialogue. Without such a dialogue leadership will be reduced to exhortation and rhetoric.

The aim of the party is to involve people in the running of their lives at every level possible. Not everyone is prepared to become a party activist. However, most people are concerned about the affairs of their village or the problems of their neighborhood. An organization that can relate to these preoccupations will find that many ordinary people will be more than ready to get involved. To do this the party has to establish special organizations that address the specific experiences of groups as varied as small peasants, youth and women.

There is no blueprint for the creation of a *special mass organization*. Each new party will have to find its own way. Instead of advocating a rigid organizational formula, the party should set about encouraging informal links. People will often do the rest. Drawing on their customs and tradition, peasants, youth or women will make suggestions as to the form of organization that corresponds to their needs. An organization that emerges as a process from real interaction and experience can spring strong roots among the masses.

The fatal flaw of the old auxiliary or mass organizations is their artificial character. Organizations that look good on paper have turned out to be alien importations to those they were meant to serve. It is far better to start off modestly and encourage local initiatives here and there, nourish them, and, step by step, build on their experience.

A party of political activists, if it is to be an agent of social transformation, has to be based on the experience of society as a whole and has to represent the totality of national life. Special mass organizations in contrast are based on specific, sometimes even sectional, interests. In the relationship between party and mass organization there must be a continuous dynamic of harmonizing the two. This can be done by extending the vision of the special mass organization through a common experience of struggle.

A party of change

Except for the small African establishment, everyone has

something to gain from the transformation of African society. Thus the party itself must be based on those who have nothing to lose and everything to gain from changing the world. It must have strong roots among workers, migrants, the landless and small peasants and clearly express the interests of these sections of society. Anyone who is prepared to join is welcome to the party. But the policies of the party have to rigidly represent the viewpoint of the dispossessed and the necessity for fundamental change.

The old parties are primarily organizations of politicians. The new party is different because its concerns are not matters of narrow political change, but the transformation of society. Such a party must be strongly linked to African youth. It is among them that an enthusiasm for change is to be found most readily. Passion, energy, idealism and a spirit of adventure are characteristics which are above all the property of youth. Young people are the most mobile, the least bound by tradition and prejudice and the most active sections of African society. That is why every important struggle on the continent has been more than anything else a movement of youth.

The party must open its doors to the youth and involve them in its activities. Most important of all, the party must learn to discipline young people without turning them into prematurely aging men and women. Discipline is necessary to give the youth direction to ensure that their energy is not dissipated in harmless outbursts. The aim of discipline is not to curb youthful passion, but to give it shape and direction. A party that can temper youthful passion with the weapon of the intellect will acquire a tremendous reservoir of energy to take on the world. A youthful party of the dispossessed is the weapon Africa needs to take on the vested interests—domestic and foreign. Such a party will not let its leaders down but will fully back them. Moreover, through its special mass organizations the party will have access to the ears of millions, who will be ready to respond to the call for action.

African leaders will get the party that they deserve. A party of change cannot be created through magic. It requires hard work and leadership. It is no exaggeration to state that the immediate test of African leadership is the question of organization. Leadership means nothing unless this problem is resolved. A collection of leaders will simply scatter in the wind at the first sign of pressure. It is only through organization that ideas acquire a practical reality and the desire for change becomes a political possibility. Organization, then, is the starting point for the creation of a new African leadership.

IV

Towards A Relevant Ideology

> *Where do correct ideas come from? Do they drop from the skies? No! Are they innate in the mind? No! They come from social practice, and from it alone. They come from three kinds of social practice: the struggle for production, the class struggle and scientific experiment. It is man's social being that determines his thought.*
>
> —Mao Zedong

Africans have every right to be suspicious of ideologies. Over the years, their leaders have all claimed that their distinct philosophy or ideology would point the way for the future. The dreams of African Socialism have turned into a nightmare and the elaborate plans have become dead letters collecting dust.

Many of the ideologies, evolved in the fifties and the sixties, were simply election promises presented in the form of philosophical statements. African politicians realized that it was easier to offer words than solve the practical problems facing their different countries. And the ideologies came thick and fast.

On the attainment of independence, the broad masses of Africa quite rightly expected far-reaching changes in their lives. No post-independence leader could ignore this widespread desire for radical change. This is why even the more moderate leaders adopted the rhetoric of radicalism and even socialism. During the sixties, one or another variant of socialism became the official philosophy of African countries. The new rulers understood that the rhetoric of socialism found a ready resonance in the aspirations of the masses. African Socialism became the respectable ideology espoused from presidential palaces up and down the continent.

With the more elitist philosophies such as that of Humanism, Authenticity and Negritude, even the radical vision is missing. Senghor's writings on Negritude are simply a restatement of African nationalism in a mystified and backward form. The main virtue of Negritude is that it means nothing specific and therefore could mean anything to anyone. For Senghor it meant above all a vain attempt to rediscover some abstract African destiny instead of practically changing the world. While Senghor went about philosophizing, his country, Senegal, remained a colony of France.

Within a few years though, it became evident that African Socialism was devoid of any practical content. It was simply a deception designed to placate mass pressure and to legitimize the authority of the new governments. The cynicism behind this ploy became clear and even fervently anti-socialist politicians like Senghor and Mboya became converts. Tom Mboya's 1965 White Paper, entitled *African Socialism and its Application to Planning in Kenya,* represented a masterstroke in duplicity. It combined a commitment to the market economy with high-sounding phrases about "pride, social justice, human dignity and political equality."

With the defeat of the mass movement and usurpation of power by the nationalist leaders, the need for a radical ideology became less pressing. African Socialism became an embarrassment to rulers totally devoted to the pursuit of private wealth. In any case, the rhetoric had become too transparent to be of any use to the leaders. Increasingly, these rulers became quiet, now and again breaking their silence on occasions like Independence Day.

Failure of the radical alternative

Not every African leader practiced the cruel deception of the Tom Mboya type. Many nationalist leaders genuinely sought radical change. Leaders like Nkrumah, Nyerere and Toure had a vision of a society where exploitation was abolished and egalitarianism and justice prevailed.

Unfortunately, the vision of even these leaders had a major defect. Their ideas were based on fine philosophical considerations but *not* on real possibilities. Nkrumah's philosophy of *Consciencism* and Nyerere's essays on *Ujamaa* showed a deep concern with the plight of their people and a desire for progress. Sadly though, their ideas were the product of their personal thinking and remained aloof from the day-to-day life of their society. Hence, their preoccupation was with what *ought* to happen, rather than with what was possible under the existing circumstances. Their vision of a new society came from their head rather than from the realities of everyday life. Visions that are not rooted firmly in the material reality remain precisely nothing more than visions.

Thus the ideas of radical leaders could have little practical consequence. Unless ideas fuse with social forces, they will not influence events nor grip the imagination of the masses. At best, they will become statements of good intentions; at worst, they will undermine the credibility of radical change. The socialist vision of radical nationalist leaders was personal rather than social, and intellectual rather than practical.

It is not surprising then that Nkrumah described *Consciencism* as a personal philosophy. Note that he advocated the need for an "intellectual revolution" as a precondition for a social one.* For indeed his ideas bear the imprint of the personal and the intellectual, rather than of social experience. The history of Africa shows that change comes about not through intellectual revolution; on the contrary, an intellectual revolution is the product of new social experience.

The strongly personal vision of African radical leaders is strikingly emphasized in the writings of Nyerere. According to him, "socialism—like democracy—is an attitude of mind".** A vision that is simply an attitude of mind is no more than wishful thinking. It is not attitudes that shape how we live, eat and work, rather it is the other way round. Even the highest ideals and the nicest attitudes cannot prevent discord if there is little to go around. That is why in Tanzania it is the struggle for survival rather than the philosophical underpinnings of *Ujamaa* that influences day-to-day existence.

The failure of the radical African alternative represented the inability of the independence politicians to evolve a strategy based on the real forces of change. Philosophies and general statements of fine principles have no practical consequences for Africans. Indeed, Cabral made a major contribution by explaining that Africa did not need more abstract ideologies but a plan of action. And he warned against the pursuit of principles which had no direct consequences for the people. As Cabral noted: "National liberation, the struggle against colonialism, the construction of peace, progress and independence are nothing but hollow words devoid of any significance unless they can be translated into a real improvement of living conditions."

*(Kwame Nkrumah: *Consciencism: Philosophy and Ideology for De-Colonization,* p. 78)
**(Julius K. Nyerere: *Ujamaa: Essays on Socialism*, p. 1)

Is and ought

Africans have had enough of philosophies and ideologies. There is no point in dreaming about what *ought* to happen. We must begin from what *is* possible. Our aim must be not to reject all dreams but to develop what *is*, what *ought* to be done. In this way new African leaders can ensure that the dilemma of the old rulers, the *separation between is and ought*, is avoided by basing their objectives on what is really practicable.

Our rejection of the utopian character of African Socialism has nothing in common with the criticism of conservative critics. Many Western and conservative observers criticize the failure of radical experiments and argue that only a market economy, based on the principle of private self-interest, can work. The Ivory Coast and Kenya are put forward as success stories of private enterprise thriving through collaboration with foreign capital. Their realism is counterposed to the failure of socialism in Sekou Toure's Guinea and Nyerere's Tanzania.

The conservative model is far from realistic. The experience of the past two decades shows that there are no private enterprise success stories. Kenya's economic decline and the collapse of Nigeria's oil revenues provide compelling cases for change. Indeed, the prospect of a booming free-enterprise Africa is just as unrealistic as the utopias of African Socialism.

The real problem that has to be tackled by Africa's new leaders is not the drawing up of a statement of aims. The real issue is how to effect change. Africa has considerable resources which at the moment are not used. The existing social organization of African countries prevents the efficient allocation of society's resources. Unless this obstacle is overcome, there will be no improvement in the life of the people.

At present the ruling classes of Africa are determined to keep things the way they are. To protect their privileges, they are quite prepared to preside over the most despicable waste of resources. The collapse of Nigerian agriculture was the result of the blind scramble for oil revenues. Instead of investing in agriculture, the Nigerian elite spent their money on luxury cars and useless gadgets.

The squandering of society's wealth, which finds a grotesque expression in the Nigerian case, shows that there is a fundamental conflict between the development of Africa's resources and its existing social organization. Africa's vast resources show the potential for development and change, but the social relations that prevail on the continent prevent the realization of this potential. This is confirmed not just in Nigeria, but in the collapse of infrastructure in the mineral-rich Shaba province of Zaire and the misuse of exceptionally fertile land in Kenya.

Once we have identified the obstacle to development in the social organization that dominates our societies, it follows that the precondition for any positive change is the removal of these social constraints. Without their removal, without a social revolution, the potential for the development of Africa will not be realized.

The impasse of African Socialism has been its failure to recognize that social revolution is the precondition for the implementation of its many fine principles. Since it attempted to introduce its ideals on society as it was, disappointment was inevitable. Even the most modest egalitarian objectives will be thwarted in a society where the market reigns supreme and where wealth is monopolized by a small clique of the rich.

It is not the lack of wealth that holds Africa back. Rather it is the way that wealth is organized and distributed. The continued misuse of this wealth indicates that the real possibilities for development are predicated on the abolition of the existing social organization of our resources. The necessity for social change, which is rooted in the material possibility for further development, has been the central lesson of African history since colonialism. Once this lesson is grasped, the dilemma that faced many of the old leaders—the separation between what is and what ought to be—will be overcome.

A theory of change

The best contribution that an African leader can make in the sphere of ideas is to take part in the development of a theory of change. This was one of the main emphases of the writings of Amilcar Cabral. As Cabral argued, "We can only truly transform our own reality on the basis of detailed knowledge of it and our own efforts and sacrifices."

The ideas that come out of the head of the isolated individual can have little effect because they are the result of private experience. Those who aspire to lead in splendid isolation have nothing to offer Africa. A quality leadership will be discovered only through an intimate acquaintance with everyday life and the experience of the masses. Such detailed knowledge is a prerequisite for recognizing what people want and how much they want it. Through this effort, those in power can learn to identify the forces of change.

In Africa at present, people live a fragmented existence divided along ethnic and class lines. As individuals we are weak and insecure, all too aware of our sense of powerlessness.

The first aim of an African leader must be to counter this through sharing the common feature of people's experience which can provide the basis for collective strength. Theory which can portray collective experience can play a major role in neutralizing divisive and conservative influences. A theory of change is a changing theory. Once an African leader has analyzed society and become acquainted with the mood and passion of the people, he can embark on the task of testing his ideas. Through engaging in a dialogue with the masses, the newly developed ideas will acquire greater immediacy and effectiveness. Once theory is taken out of the hands of the individual, it itself becomes the product of society. The new leader will have to be forceful and modest at the same time— he will have to teach and to learn. No one is so farsighted that he can do without learning from his people.

A theory of change that accords with real life is the point of departure for the new Africa. Such a theory will cease to be a set of ideas and become a force for change. But there is still more at stake. Through the process of developing a people-oriented theory, the new African leader will be formed. The fight to develop and test new ideas will shape and mold the type of leader that is genuinely the product of the society yearning for change.

"But what about the blueprint for the future?" demand our young African friends. It is very easy to invent blueprints. But a new society cannot be invented. It has to be fought for. It will arise out of the struggle that is still ahead. Instead of offering reassuring plans about the future, the new leader could better employ his energies learning about the barriers to change.

The people of Africa can live without blueprints. They want a society where their modest ambitions for a decent life can become a reality. At present even the most modest aspirations of our people remain unfulfilled. The obstacles to further progress are many. But these obstacles can be overcome through leadership devoted to change. The present social organization was not created by nature; it was created by people. It can also be dismantled by people.

Finally, a theory of change cannot be developed by individuals who are immune to change themselves. It is the height of arrogance for Africa's present leaders to imagine that they can change Africa and maintain themselves the way they are. Unless leaders are prepared to change themselves, learn the spirit of sacrifice and acquire the strength that comes from collective action, they will play no role in the creation of a new society. An African theory of change, based on the continent's experience of struggle, will itself become a most powerful inspiration for a new world.

V

Forces for Change

The self-sufficient independent producer has been replaced by the half-peasant and half-proletariat in Africa. With one foot on the land and the other in the towns, this social group has become increasingly mobile and conscious and therefore capable of advocating and supporting radical change ... The secret of African liberation lies in activating this as yet silent majority. Together with its allies in the towns, this rural force represents a powerful combination capable of transforming Africa.

There is little point in discussing the need for a relevant ideology or the necessity for a party for change unless it is possible to show that within African society as it now exists there are discernible forces for social tranformation. This is no small problem, for without the existence of identifiable agents for change all ideas about a liberated future become a harmless utopia. The agents for change, the revolutionary classes can be found in the often complex structures of African society.

At first sight the task of locating the agency of radical transformation in African society appears to be daunting. In Africa classes have developed in their own special way and no ready-made model can make sense of this unique social mosaic.

Social development is often uneven. But in the colonial era a distorted form of evolution ensured that the pattern of uneven development was profoundly consolidated and regional differences became exceptionally pronounced. Consequently, the impact of change as it affected classes has been often restricted to limited geographical areas. In certain parts of Africa the introduction of the market has speeded up class differentiation while elsewhere it appears that little has changed and time has stood still. New classes closely linked with commercial and productive activities directed at the world market exist in the same African nation with people whose way of life is still dominated by the exigencies of a subsistence economy.

The patterns of uneven development have also shaped the complexion of the elite. The Westernized businessman or civil servant appears to have little in common with the landowner or the religious leader in the hinterland. Common strands of interest which unite landowner and civil servant into class are far from apparent as regional or cultural differences appear to predominate. Looked at from this perspective the prospects seem to be more for regional rivalries rather than for thorough-going change. Where in this context are the agents for social change to be found?

The paradox of the independent peasant

Of any region in the Third World, Africa stands out as the continent of the independent peasant. In contrast to Latin America, South-East Asia or the Middle East the polarization of landownership between large estate and small holdings is much less developed in Africa. Those totally without claim to any form of land form a relatively small proportion of the

African rural population. Consequently a larger percentage of African peasants cultivate their own land than in most parts of the Third World.

The independent subsistence-oriented peasant forms the backbone of African society. Historically, this group has tended to play a relatively conservative role. Bound to the land and isolated from the rest of society, the outlook of the peasant tends to be parochial and fiercely resistant to change. Such attitudes are entirely understandable since change has generally been at the peasants' expense.

In fact, it is far too simplistic to view the African peasant as an undifferentiated mass. Cotton farmers in Buganda or cocoa farmers in Ghana are often rural entrepreneurs employing the labor of others. The prosperous Chagga coffee farmers in Tanzania have little in common with the landless Kikuyu in Kenya. Not only is social differentiation in the African countryside a reality but it is also accelerating at a fast pace.

There can be little doubt that the foundations for the independent subsistence-oriented peasant are being eroded. Peasants have for some time reorientated their activities towards the production of cash crops and have found meeting their subsistence requirements a real challenge. Insofar as peasants have retained their independence, it has not been as subsistence farmers but as cash crop cultivators.

But in reality it is the very independence of the African peasantry that is under question. Lack of investment, the growth of cash-cropping and population increases have all put considerable pressure on the land. Soil erosion and drought conditions in large parts of Africa show that the material foundations for an independent peasantry are precarious.

Famine is only the most extreme expression of the crisis

facing the African peasant. For some time now in many parts of Africa peasants have found that their landholdings are insufficient to meet the requirements of subsistence. At the same time for most there is no realistic alternative to trying to make a living on one's plot. Jobs in the city are few and only available to those fortunate enough to have a high level of education or good contacts. Even if more jobs were available most peasants would think twice before they irrevocably cut their ties with the only economic security available to them—their land.

In practice most peasants have attempted to resolve the problem of survival by holding onto their land and also seeking job opportunities elsewhere. Labor migration on a vast scale throughout Africa is in part a response to a system of landholding which cannot provide permanent jobs. The African peasantry is in a state of disintegration and a significant section of this social group can be more precisely characterized as half-peasant and half-migrant laborer. The conservation of small holdings in fact obscures the process whereby survival can only be secured by means other than peasant production. From this perspective, instead of being *independent* the African peasant can be seen as *dependent,* or more accurately as semi-proletarianized. It only requires one drought season for the myth of the independent peasant to be cruelly exposed.

The changes experienced by the rural population in Africa are far-reaching—not even the remotest part of the continent remains immune to them. It is these changes that make significant sections of the peasantry a force for change. African peasants confronted with the problem of survival are no longer constituents of isolated communities. Millions have migrated in search of jobs intermingling with those from other regions. In the cities, mines and plantations short-term migrants from many parts of Africa work alongside each other and acquire an understanding of life not available to their grandparents who left the villages infrequently. An outlook based on broad experiences of life characterizes the semi-proletarianized section of the rural population.

With tenuous links to the land and little stake in urban society as it is now constituted, the rural proletariat has emerged as a force for change. More than any section of society this social group can have no future without the transformation of society. The rural proletariat shares with urban workers a freedom from property. Neither has property and both live entirely from the earnings of their labor. In recent times the rural proletariat has not even enjoyed the security of work available to those in permanent wage labor.

The self-sufficient independent producer has been replaced by the half-peasant and half-proletariat of Africa. With one foot on the land and the other in the towns this social group has become increasingly mobile and conscious and therefore capable of advocating and supporting radical change. The conservative layers in the countryside, such as landlords and prosperous cash-crop entrepreneurs, still exercise considerable influence, but for a significant section of rural Africa there is little worth conserving. The secret of African liberation lies in activating this as yet silent majority. Together with its allies in the towns this rural force represents a powerful combination capable of transforming Africa.

If the rural communities have the numbers then the urban areas have the education and expertise necessary for ensuring that the silent majority finds its voice and sense of purpose. At the same time without the social weight of the rural poor the urban working masses and intellectuals lack the power to effectively challenge the status quo. This potentially complimentary relationship will not emerge spontaneously. It requires hard work and organization.

Organizing the peasantry and the rural proletariat is one of the most pressing challenges of our time. It is a challenge that has too often been ignored by African political leaders. Politics is generally treated as the preserve of urban politicians. The countryside is used as a stage army and only the rural establishment is ever consulted. The job facing the party of change is to appeal directly to the peasantry. This requires the establishment of new organizations in the countryside which assist the evolution of the rural proletariat as a political force. The party of change ought to learn from the experience of Latin America and Asia where peasant movements have acquired activists. Rural education, cooperative organizations and peasant unions can make an important contribution in politicizing the countryside. Such institutions help transcend the isolation of rural communities and make the rural poor aware of their common experience and collective power. A perspective that focuses on revitalizing the countryside is essential for shaking up the existing urban oriented politics of the elite. The *status quo* can only be maintained if the rural communities are fragmented and apathetic. When the majority is no longer silent Africa will embark on the road to change.

VI

On Organizing Africa's Wealth

What is important is that agriculture develops in line with domestic needs. Just as agriculture can stimulate industry, so the other way around. The priority of industry should be to produce the tools, machines and other inputs which African farmers require to make the land prosper.

An industry based on agriculture can minimize Africa's reliance on the world market and ensure that the rhythm of its development is consistent with available resources. In the last analysis, Africa, as the radical economic adage goes, must produce what it consumes and consume what it produces.

Africa is in the midst of a monumental economic catastrophe. The hunger that stalks the continent spares no nation. Even her most successful Westernized cities— Nairobi, Lagos, Accra—are surrounded by the sprawling shantytowns of the poor and hungry. African leaders have given up trying; only the dictates of the IMF and foreign banks give economic policy a semblance of coherence. Governments have simply lost control of the continent's wealth. Even the richest of her nations—Nigeria, Ivory Coast, Kenya—are facing economic disaster. Mineral-rich Zaire is now virtually owned by foreign banks. Unless today's leaders reclaim her wealth and set about constructing the economy for the people, Africa, as it is presently known, will cease to exist. If Africans are unable to sustain themselves, there will be no scope for political change and no potential for the realization of African leadership.

Economics of despair

In 1978, Edem Kodjo, former Secretary-General of the Organization of African Unity, told a group of African leaders that "Africa is dying":

If things continue as they are, only eight or nine of the present countries will survive the next few years. All other things being equal, absolute poverty, instead of decline, is likely to gain ground. It is clear that the economy of our continent is lying in ruins. . . . Our ancient continent is now on the brink of disaster.

That was in 1978. Since then the situation has gone from bad to worse. The horrors of mass starvation in Ethiopia and Sudan have received widespread publicity. But the famine is not confined to the arid Sahel region. The World Bank's 1984 report classified 24 of Africa's 39 sub-Saharan states as "MSA"—"most seriously affected" by famine. In any *normal* year, 100 million Africans—a fifth of the continent's population—are close to death from lack of food. Twenty of the 36 poorest countries in the world are in Africa. In plain language, it means that 70 out of every 100 Africans are destitute.

The situation is getting worse all the time. Overall food output in Africa has fallen one percent per year during the last 15 years. Hence, food production is falling behind the growth of population and in most African countries food consumption per head is less today than it was in 1970. At present, more than 20 African countries are faced with major food shortages.

Statistics throw light on the scale of Africa's agricultural disaster. But the human cost is not so easily quantifiable. Mass impoverishment dominates everyday life, leading to the erosion of our social fabric and the upheaval of our continent. While some move about searching for food, millions are fleeing into the cities. Tragically, there is no easy escape from destitution. Millions of Africans living in urban areas walk the streets without hope of ever finding decent employment.

The degradation and despair of Africans imposes a grave responsibility on their leaders. Change there must be, but to succeed we must know what has gone wrong.

Western squeeze

There are many causes of Africa's economic decline. Governments have squandered the continent's wealth and sold it to the highest bidder. The economics of greed have influenced the way Africa's resources have been invested and distributed. The economics of greed know no political or national allegiances. The ruling class of so-called socialist Tanzania, like their counterparts in capitalist Nigeria, understand only the language of profit. They have not done badly at all. While 43 percent of the children of Tanzania and 16 percent of Nigeria's suffer from malnutrition, the fat cats gloat over their Western bank accounts.

The greatest crime of the leaders has been their betrayal of Africa to foreign interests. Little has changed since the days of colonialism. Throughout this century capitalist development in Africa has been shaped by the West's plunder of its vast natural wealth. During the colonial period the West turned Africa into a source of cheap raw materials and foodstuffs and a market for their products. Africa's post-independence leaders have been happy to continue with this state of affairs. As a result, Africa's resources and the fruits of its labor continue to flow to the West. Most profits generated in Africa are syphoned off by Western banks and investors.

In return for a comfortable life, African leaders have directed the continent's economy to serve foreign interests. Concentrating on producing raw material for exports, Africa has become entirely dependent on Western markets. The very existence of the majority of Africans depends on economic forces entirely out of their control. Africa produces what external economic forces ask of her, in quantities and at a price set by them. African needs are only incidental considerations when it comes to economic affairs.

Africa is a permanent hostage to Western markets. From a position of weakness Africans have to accept the fact that the Western economic forces pay less for their products now than a decade ago. Africa's industry and agriculture, starved of resources, are near collapse. The harder Africa works and the more it sells abroad, the more it falls into debt.

There are two immediate causes of the African disaster: falling world prices of raw materials and rising debts. Between 1973 and 1982 the purchasing power of African exports fell by 20 percent, and it has fallen faster since. In 1983 the prices of cobalt, copper and coffee fell by 50, 20 and 40 percent respectively. The collapse of world prices has had a devastating impact on economies which depend on the export of a small range of primary products. Ghana, for example, has been plunged into a crisis as the price of cocoa fell by 70 percent between 1978 and 1983. As the price of Africa's exports fell, the continent received less back in return. Africa has been forced to send more and more of its resources abroad and eventually to starve millions of its people.

The most recent Sahel famine began in 1983. But in 1983-84, five Sahelian countries—Burkina Faso, Mali, Niger, Senegal and Chad—harvested a record 154 million tons of cotton fibre. In Mali food production declined by 50 percent in the 70s, but cotton production increased almost four-fold. The same process occurred in Ethiopia: while peasants starved, investment in the land was directed towards the production of coffee exports. To compensate for falling prices, African countries have turned a growing proportion of arable land over to producing cash crops for export. Meanwhile agriculture has been starved of funds and technology. Famine and starvation are the direct consequence.

Trade is not the only way that the West plunders Africa. Through the receipt of foreign loans, the future of Africa has been virtually mortgaged to Western banks. Africa has a higher level of debt than anywhere else in the world. It stands at 58 percent of Africa's annual product. Servicing this debt consumes almost a third of her earnings from exports and services. In 1984, Western banks extracted a staggering $11 billion in interest payments from the starving continent. The African famine is certainly not bad business for Western banks.

Africa's debt gives Western nations enormous powers over her affairs. Since the late seventies, the IMF and World Bank have forced African governments to impose severe austerity measures on the masses. The West has made currency devaluations and food subsidy cuts a precondition for extending African debt payment, and for providing aid. As a result, hunger, scarcity and disease have become even more pervasive.

There is resentment but no effective action against Western banks and the IMF. The July 1985 annual conference of the Organization of African Unity (OAU) typically adopted the sycophantic approach. Meeting in the capital of poverty-stricken Ethiopia, the African leaders thanked Western donors for the food aid they received and implored the banks for some relief from the onerous conditions imposed by the IMF.

It is clear that foreign debt has provided Western powers with the pretext to informally recolonize the continent. Western advisors do more than advise—they are in Africa to dictate terms. As one unusually frank official of the World Bank indicated recently, "we are talking about a kind of recolonization which means sending back white boys to tell them how to run their countries."

The Western squeeze is on. African governments made up of collaborators have become accomplices to a new kind of enslavement of the continent. While millions of Africans face starvation, the Western banks are reaping a rich harvest. The only answer to the African famine is to liberate the continent so that its resources can finally be used by the African people to whom they belong.

Reclaiming Africa's wealth: a plan of action

Africa is rich, endowed with all the resources necessary for a good productive life. Even areas considered to be the poorest can sustain a prosperous existence. For example the World Bank states that famine-ridden Ethiopia has enough land to support a population of 310 million—ten times the present population! It is not nature that has been unkind to the continent. Famine and poverty are the result of insidious forces which have turned Africa into the backyard of Western powers.

Where should we start? The vast majority of Africans still live on the land. There can be no progress unless the agrarian problem is solved and Africa is able once again to feed itself. Land could thrive if Africans started investing in it instead of only exploiting it so that they can sell more cash crops abroad for a lower price.

The funds for investing in land are available. The billions of dollars that are taken away from the people as payment for interest on external debt could have a dramatic effect on agricultural development if they were invested in the land. Natural justice must have priority over the profits of Western banks. In any case, the West has bled Africa dry for decades. By any standard of morality they ought now begin to compensate Africa for the billions that were stolen from it.

The cancellation of foreign debt is a precondition for establishing control over the development of her resources. Africans don't want charity, just their birthright. Ridding Africa of the scourge of Western bankers is just the first step to establishing a new African economic order.

Agricultural production must be redirected from serving the world market to meeting domestic need. Food production, the realization of subsistence needs, must precede any other agricultural activities. This is not a matter of choice but of necessity. Investment must be directed to food production. If necessary, land used for export crops must be reallocated for the purpose of food production. There is plenty of land available for cultivation. It should be made available to all who want to work on the land. With modest outlays of investment, Africa's peasants could produce enough to feed themselves and their families. To realize this objective, all land should be nationalized and redistributed to those who are prepared to grow food.

Only after the domestic food requirements have been met should land be given over to the production of export crops. Indeed, the emphasis should not be on producing for the world market but for domestic industry. Africa has little control over what it sells on the world market. It makes more sense to produce raw materials that domestic industry can use. This way Africans can retain more control over the products of their labor and also assist the development of their industry.

The production of cash crops should be regulated through state-run marketing boards. These boards should be responsible not only for the marketing of crops but also for ensuring that production takes place in line with the nation's priorities for agriculture. A board's pricing policy should reflect this concern and resources should be distributed in accordance with the priority of long-term agrarian development. To be effective, the marketing boards must be supported by laws directed towards the curbing of unregulated commercial activities. Insofar as private traders assist the network of distribution their contribution should be welcomed, but antisocial and parasitic activities should be forcefully discouraged.

The potential for development varies from country to country. What is important is that agriculture develops in line with domestic needs. To feed the population African countries can easily afford to forego the dubious privilege of earning a few dollars for their exports. If this strategy is pursued consistently then agriculture can provide the raw materials around which industry can flourish. An industry based on agriculture can minimize its reliance on the world market and ensure that the rhythm of its development is consistent with available resources.

Just as agriculture can stimulate industry, so the other way around. The priority of industry should be to produce the tools, machines and other inputs which African farmers require to make the land prosper. An industrial sector that is oriented towards agriculture will have no problems about finding customers. Millions of peasants need everything from simple tools to irrigation equipment. With such equipment farmers will be able to achieve levels of production which today would be considered a miracle.

Africa will not become prosperous overnight. But if a harmonious relationship is established between agriculture and industry, at least Africans will be able to employ everyone in productive work. Eradicating the fundamental problems of starvation and unemployment is far preferable to the present state of affairs. Africans might invoke the wrath of Western powers but that is a small price to pay for reclaiming the dignity and creativity of the people.

This strategy for change is no utopian fantasy. In many parts of Africa it could be implemented with little effort, elsewhere it will require a major act of will. Oil and mineral rich nations such as Zaire and Nigeria could easily redirect their revenues to an agriculture-based strategy of development. They would simply need to redirect their resources from the present unproductive and Western-dominated sectors to productive domestic agriculture and industry. Other countries such as Kenya, Zimbabwe or the Ivory Coast already have the resources to implement the new strategy. Elsewhere, for example in the Sahelian countries, it will take much struggle and a considerable period to reverse the present decline.

Reclaiming Africa's wealth is not a narrow economic matter. It requires bold leadership to challenge vested interests, both domestic and external, which have no interest in change. It requires determination to take on foreign interests who benefit from the enslavement of Africa.

The implementation of Africa's plan for action is devastatingly simple. But establishing the right political climate for its promotion is not. African capitalists and Western bankers will not accept any fundamental change for the economy. They will fight tooth and nail against any attempt to reclaim Africa's wealth. That is why questions such as agrarian change and industrial development are ultimately reducible to politics. A change in the political climate can have far-reaching effects. Once Western influence is removed Africa can turn towards solving its problems on a continental basis. Nothing is more rational than a division of labor that embraces the continent. At present Africa is turned on itself through bitter rivalries. If African countries could learn to cooperate with each other then all could benefit. Western powers could no longer play one African country off against another and the influence of foreign interests would be severely reduced.

There are major opportunities for the strengthening of economic links within the continent. At present, economic relations between African countries are minimal. African nations are locked into the international division of labor as isolated individual units. This external orientation counteracts even the most modest attempts at self-reliance. The collapse of the East African Economic Community illustrates the fragility of regional cooperation. Yet the future of Africa lies not with the Lomé Convention, the EEC or the Francophone Bloc. Regional cooperation and trade is a precondition for any successful developmental policy. Instead of dealing from the position of weakness that characterizes Africa's trade with the West, regional trade can be carried out on the basis of equality. Many of the disadvantages of international trade, such as access to hard currency, can be avoided through inter-African relations.

Trade policy should give preference first to Africa-to-Africa and second to Africa-and-South links. Closer links with other regions of the South makes good economic sense. It is also essential for reversing the existing patterns of economic domination on the world market. Through such cooperation, Africa and the South in general can neutralize some of the negative effects of a Western-dominated world economy. Wherever possible Africa should insist on barter or countertrade arrangements to free itself from the currency and credit regulations that are used to thwart its economic independence.

Trade with the West has to be carefully regulated to counteract its potentially invidious consequences. It is not enough to prevent the importation of luxury goods. What is required is a monopoly over foreign trade which regulates both what is bought and what is sold to the world market. Only with such a monopoly can the state be in a position to direct the distribution of the nation's resources. In this way, the resources of the nation can be sold with the express purpose of purchasing technology essential for the realization of developmental priorities. Wherever possible the Eastern Bloc should be used as a trading partner so as to put pressure on Western firms to grant major concessions.

Although Africa-wide cooperation is the long term objective, Africans must start where they can. Every nation can start on the road to prosperity if it stands up to foreign interests. Economic change cannot come about piecemeal. The basic structures of the capitalist market divert resources towards areas which serve the pockets of a handful of exploiters. The market knows no morality. For profiteers a famine is just another opportunity to line their pockets. The misery of millions provides the rich with fabulous wealth. While hundreds of thousands go hungry, rich traders hoard maize in Kenya. The only morality of the market is to make sure that the rich get richer and the poor get poorer. The market is the disease and starvation one of its symptoms.

Instead of the principle of the market, Africa should put to the fore the principle of need. Her resources must serve her needs. Common sense alone tells us that the needs of Africa should come before anything else. Only those who benefit from the exploitation of others can possibly object. Taking away the fruits of what others produced has not served Africa well. That is why Africans need a society based on common need and not private greed. Africa's future depends on reclaiming Africa's wealth now.

VII

On Building a Nation
Devoid of Ethnic Conflicts

You may be surprised to know that we consider the contradictions between the tribes a secondary one. . . . We consider that there are many more contradictions between what you might call the economic tribes in the capitalist countries than there are between the ethnic tribes in Guinea. . . .

Structural, organizational and other measures must be taken to ensure that this contradiction does not explode and become a more important contradiction. . . .

Our struggle for national liberation and the work done by our Party have shown that this contradiction is really not so important. . . .

As soon as we organized the liberation struggle properly the contradiction between the tribes proved to be a feeble, secondary contradiction.

—Amilcar Cabral

Economic decline threatens the very existence of the African nation. Bitter competition over scarce resources has provided a focus for the escalation of ethnic conflicts. Regional conflicts have led to civil wars which often spread across national boundaries. Hunger breeds strife and no

59

African nation is immune from the scourge of ethnic rivalries. Every government in Africa is all too aware of its failure to give the concept of nationhood more than a semblance of reality.

The myth of tribalism

The all-pervasive character of ethnic disputes has given rise to the view that tribalism is a natural feature of Africa. African leaders are so steeped in ethnic considerations that they cannot imagine any other mode of operation. Indeed it is now commonplace to reduce every aspect of political life to the tribal factor. Can it really be so? And what are the roots of this strange African affliction?

Ethnic consciousness is by no means peculiar to African societies. Throughout the world peasant societies evolved distinct customs, cultures and dialects. As a rule, it can be said that the less developed societies are, the stronger the local bonds that differentiate regions from each other. Peasants and herdsmen working alongside each other depend on mutual help in the struggle for survival. Living a relatively isolated existence, parochial identity is reinforced and outsiders are looked upon with a mixture of fear and suspicion. Many of these sentiments continue after peasants have moved off the land and into the cities. Thus newly urbanized peasants in 18th century Paris settled among kinsmen from their region of origin. The persistence of regional identity even in an urban environment, is evident throughout Europe in the 19th century.

So Africa has no monopoly over ethnic consciousness. Nor is it necessarily a problem. What is a problem is when ethnic consciousness is transformed into a hostile prejudice directed against other people. This transformation is one of the main legacies of the colonial period.

During the colonial period Africa was divided arbitrarily into a series of artificial units. Some ethnic units found themselves living on different sides of the colonial border. Inside the new colonial boundaries different ethnic groups were thrown together and ruled by a single administration. The colonial system brought different ethnic groups together so as to divide them more than ever before.

The main administrative principle of colonialism was the policy of divide and rule. Some ethnic groups were drawn into the colonial economy, others were relegated to the role of migrant workers, while still others on the margins of society were left to stagnate. In most colonies the administrators picked one ethnic group for special attention. For example, the Baganda upper class were chosen by the British in Uganda as allies with limited privileges. Colonial development was fundamentally uneven, reinforcing regional and ethnic differences. The colonial authorities understood that it was easier to control a dozen ethnic groups than a united people. To safeguard its system, the colonial regime pursued a policy directed towards ethnic hostilities. Colonial government endeavored to recruit soldiers from one ethnic group and officers from another. The civil service and other employers followed the same pattern and recruited along ethnic lines. In West Africa, the British administration recruited officers from the southern regions while lower ranks were taken from the less developed areas of the north. In Uganda, the relatively prosperous Baganda were virtually excluded from the army in favor of the less educated people in the north. In Kenya, the colonial administration sought to ensure that the police were drawn from a different ethnic group than the one being policed.

The policy of divide and rule was designed not only to isolate one ethnic group from another but also to set them against each other. In Uganda the British regime sent Baganda tax collectors and officials to the northern areas just as in Ghana, southern officials—Asante, Fanti, and Ewe— were posted up north. In northern Nigeria, most of the teachers and civil servants were Ibos from the east. The aim was to ensure that local anger would be directed at the Ibo civil servants and not at the colonial regime.

To counter the emerging nationalist movement, the colonial authorities did their best to fan the flames of ethnic discord. In many colonies, national political parties were made illegal and parties were forced to organize on a regional basis. In Guinea, the French administration organized Fulani leaders to oppose the nationalist movement, and in Zaire, colonial influence succeeded in destroying the liberation movement and fragmenting it along ethnic lines. Although Zaire was an extreme case, no nationalist movement succeeded in effectively countering the invidious effect of the policy of divide and rule. The bloody civil wars in Sudan, Nigeria, Uganda, Zaire and Burundi are a testimony to the persistence of colonial influence.

Like the famine that devastates Africa, tribalism does not spring from the African soil. Tribalism is a colonial creation which now haunts the African way of life. But why should this foreign implantation acquire a growing momentum with the passing of time?

The hidden tribe

Instead of fighting the policy of divide and rule, our leaders have capitulated to it. All the colonial institutions which were based on the policy of divide and rule were happily inherited by the incoming governments.

The nationalist movements were often little more than an alliance of regional leaders. As long as it was a question of winning independence, this alliance could be more or less sustained. But after independence matters took a turn for the worse. Leading politicians sought to strengthen their position by consolidating their links with their region of origin. Those in power could afford to declare their loyalty to the nation state. Those politicians excluded from effective power sought compensation in building a base of support in their regions. Since the national governments were busy rewarding their own supporters anyway, opposition politicians could easily present their own exclusion from power as an insult to their region.

The nationalist movement quickly disintegrated. Too often, the former nationalist statesman turned into a regional boss. It was all very easy—the structures of the colonial system were at hand to lend legitimacy to regional organization and regional consciousness.

Most nationalist leaders never entirely broke from regional connections. After independence, as political competition became more intense, party leaders scrambled to establish their regional base of support. Going back to the regions was easier and a safer bet than forging a national forum for political discussion and competition. Debate and the fight for political leadership in the national arena became increasingly irrelevant. What mattered was the regional support that party leaders could mobilize to back up their claims for national power.

It is the narrow self-interest of our political leaders that is responsible for the crisis of African nationhood. In the colonial period tribalism was an effective policy of divide and rule. In the post-colonial era tribalism became the main vehicle for the achievement of political power and of social mobility. "By whatever means necessary" was the principle of political ambition. Since the colonial era, every frustrated politician has rediscovered his ethnic roots. The most Westernized leaders educated in Europe and North America now make a living out of promoting ethnic differences.

Writers and journalists glibly talk of tribal conflict. But many of these conflicts have no bases in African history. Tribal conflicts bear the stamp of political competition within the ruling class. It is the rich and powerful who pursue tribalism as a way of life. The secession of Katanga (now Shaba province) from Zaire was not the product of mass ethnic hostility but the manipulation of Tshombe and his business friends. In Kenya it was the African representatives of multinational companies who organized a "mass oathing" campaign among the Kikuyu people directed against other ethnic groups. We can see the same cynical maneuvers in South Africa today. The first concern of Chief Buthelezi, whenever he returns from his business trips to Israel and Europe, is to foster Zulu consciousness and hatred for other African people. As a "tribal millionaire" Buthelezi understands that ethnic hostility is a profitable source of power and privilege.

The tragedy that faces Africa is that our rulers have succeeded in drawing millions of ordinary people behind the ethnic banner. In their day-to-day existence most Africans have little scope of being tribalistic. But when the tribal network is the only route for gaining access to the ears of civil servants and politicians, even ordinary Africans become all too conscious of the importance of their ethnic identity. That is why political and economic conflict can often assume an ethnic form.

The real tribalists of course are the ruling classes, everyone else the victims. In reality, ruling class tribalists are not preoccupied with their ethnic identity. They mix with each other at Western embassy parties. Despite their fervent advocacy of ethnic traditions, they are not in the least bit inhibited about sending their children to Western schools abroad. In the cities they lead a comfortable Western-style life. It is only when they go back to their regions that these elites assume the mantle of ethnic tradition. There they work hard to make sure that the people do not forget their ethnic identity for one minute. Ironically, the only tribe that counts is hidden from the public view. Ruling class tribalists are drawn from across ethnic lines and have a common interest in perpetuating regional hostility and conflict.

The two tribes

In Africa there are two tribes—the exploiters and the exploited, the rulers and the ruled. African political leaders have succeeded in obscuring this central fact of life. By fomenting discord between different ethnic groups, workers and peasants have been set against each other instead of fighting their exploiters. Tribalism has become a most powerful ideological weapon for perpetuating exploitation.

The new generation of African leaders cannot reconcile themselves to the problem of ethnic rivalries. Precisely because tribal identity has been artificially matured it can be fought. A genuine party of change can find its own way of showing how all African workers and peasants, regardless of their ethnic origins, have a common interest in getting rid of the tribal millionaires. This is not a matter of faith but of practical reality. Workers and peasants are first of all part of the same class. It is this common experience of being exploited that marks them apart from their exploiters. The tribal leaders may speak a similar dialect as their followers, but they lead a different life and their privileges are made possible directly at the expense of their people. It is the task of a party of change to expose this fundamental conflict of interest between the two tribes. The best antidote to tribalism is the politics of class.

The deep wound inflicted by the tribal scourge will not heal quickly. African governments must become sensitive to ethnic identity and differences in culture and custom. The validity of ethnic identity can be recognized while combatting the manipulation of this identity towards hostile ends. Indeed, it is through defending the rights of every ethnic group and fighting ethnic exclusiveness that a party of change can demonstrate the common bond that unites all workers and all peasants.

The party itself must set the example. It must be a truly national party of workers and peasants involving people from all regions. The party leadership itself has to make every effort to promote people from all ethnic groups into its ranks. By setting an example, the party can act as a living proof that all Africans, regardless of ethnic background, can work and cooperate with each other towards a common objective.

The program of the party must decisively take into account the reality of ethnic tensions—not to provoke them but to minimize them. The program must pay special attention to those ethnic groups that have hitherto been excluded from influence or who have suffered discrimination from the central government. The party must bend the stick in favor of these sections of society. Only in this way will it be possible to overcome the fears and suspicions of those people that have faced the hostile oppression of the establishment.

Economic resources have to be distributed equitably without regard to ethnic considerations. Every region must have a say about its own future development. There will always be backward politicians who will seek to provoke ethnic tensions but if Africa's leadership is seen to be acting in the interest of the nation there will be no room for the pursuit of tribal manipulation.

In the urban areas the party has considerable potential for organizing across ethnic lines from the start. Mobilizing workers and migrants towards clearly defined social objectives, the party can create a new identity based on shared experience of class. To counter ethnic institutions in the cities, the party should establish special projects which are run by and cater to all. Projects offering assistance on health, education, housing, industrial matters and legal aid can provide a forum where people from all ethnic groups come in contact with each other and learn about each other's lives. Public meetings, entertainment, party press and propaganda are useful instruments for stimulating a truly national outlook.

The crisis of African nationhood can only be resolved by the united struggle of workers and peasants. Only these classes have an interest in destroying the ethnic divisions that are destroying the African continent. The ruling class tribalists on the other hand, desperately cling to their ethnic base. Appeals for cooperation will not work. Only when class politics prevail will the African nation be resurrected.

VIII

On The African State Machine

The African state today tends to represent the narrow concerns of the privileged elite. That is why the neocolonial state has such close affinity with international interests. . . . The creation of a new state requires the establishment of a popular counter-institution through which the masses can exert control over their own lives.

For most Africans the state is an alien and hostile institution. The state never gives—it always takes. It never inquires or asks—the state demands and gives orders. The representatives of the state, be they civil servants or policemen, first threaten and then ponder how much they can get from you. Unless they are dealing with the rich, their humiliating manner always indicates that they are doing you a favor. No wonder that, whenever possible, Africans seek to avoid any direct contact with the state.

Whatever the form of government, there is little to distinguish between the different African states. Between the military rulers of Nigeria or Ghana and the one-party states of Kenya and Malawi, the only difference is in the clothes that the leaders wear. The so-called multiparty states of Senegal or Gambia are no less aloof from the population than those of their neighbors.

The unrepresentative state

The origins of the modern African state lie in the colonial period. The colonial regime established a bureaucracy, military and police force to enforce its interests. The colonial administration was an alien implantation designed to defend foreign interests in Africa. The state apparatus was organized in line with the requirements of the colonial power. Hence it was responsive not to local needs but to the dictates of Whitehall or the Elysée Palace. The state was accountable to none other than the foreign powers it served. The main feature of the colonial state was that it made no pretense of representing African people; its sole role was to administer the "natives."

This was the state apparatus that African nationalist leaders took over after the end of the colonial era. In all its essentials the state apparatus survived the transfer of government power. Unlike the old colonial masters, the nationalist leaders had strong direct links with the African population. But the state machine that they tried to use to implement new policies remained the same. To say that the state machine was out of touch with the aspirations of independent Africa is an understatement. The expatriate civil servants retained the arrogance of the old colonial masters and carried on as before. The African civil servants were drawn from the most privileged section of the local population. Well educated and imbued with strong Western values they shared the Europeans' contempt for the African way of life. The military were sheltered from the struggle for survival that faced most Africans and the officer corps assimilated the outlook and values of the Western institutions that trained them.

The state machine that the African leaders took over was organized and run on principles which were fundamentally antithetical to the dreams and objectives of the nationalist movement. The question that was posed throughout Africa was: would the state imprison the nationalist politicians or would the new leaders master the state machine and use it in the interest of society? The depressing answer soon became evident. Nationalist leaders proved incapable of transforming the state apparatus; instead, they themselves were transformed into captives of the administrative machine.

The domestication and neutralization of nationalist leaders by the state apparatus represented a devastating blow to the dreams of the movement for independence. But there was a problem with even more far-reaching consequences.

The newly independent African countries were left with economies that could barely sustain the existing level of living standards. There was little scope for economic and social development. Industry and agriculture were relatively weak and showed little potential for the generation of wealth. Only one institution stood out as stable and powerful—and that was the state. In economic terms, the state emerged as the dominant force in African society. It was the largest single employer of labor. It had access to domestic resources and investment funds from abroad. The state was not only an institution of administration, but also the most powerful economic force in society.

Since the middle classes—traders and businessmen—were relatively weak, economic success was contingent on access to the resources of the state. Soon everyone realized that the only road to prosperity ran through the state machine.

The emergence of the state as the main engine of economic development had important implications for African politics and administration. Civil servants and bureaucrats soon realized that employment in the public sector bestowed important privileges on them. In conditions of scarcity, access to licenses, contracts or leases was a much sought after commodity. Having a contract in the civil service was essential for every businessman or trader. Even the distribution of scholarships for places of higher education could be turned to advantage by government servants.

Nationalist leaders soon understood that political influence was synonymous with economic power, and without the backing of the state none could pursue a successful career in business. That is why every ambitious politician and businessman fought desperately to carve out a place for themselves inside the state apparatus. With so much at stake, none could afford to give up their influence with the state machine.

In the West, businessmen and politicians can afford to lose elections and spend a period in opposition. They can return to running their businesses or other enterprises. But when there are no avenues to prestige and wealth outside the state, an election becomes an all-or-nothing gamble. In Africa, the loss of influence over the state means the loss of everything. The ruling class in Africa cannot maintain its power and prestige without directly running the state.

It is because the state is so important for sustaining the rich and the influential that it has become such a battleground. The state is not only an apparatus of administration, but the arena where most of the competition between sections of the ruling class takes place. Since even the resources of the state are insufficient for filling the capacious appetite of the rich, the conflict within this institution is always intense, bordering on war.

We can now better understand the disease of one-party states and military *coups*. Parliamentary democracy, or indeed any kind of democracy, is a luxury that the African ruling class cannot afford. No African government can countenance the loss of office. Losing an election means not only the end of political influence, but also the termination of the only access to economic resources.

It is the unique role of the African state as the main source of economic and political power that explains virtually everything about political life in recent decades. At the first opportunity every political leader declares a fervent commitment to the one-party state. The justifications are many— the purpose is clear. A one-party system eliminates rivals for influence and consolidates the hold of the governing party over the state. The leaders hope that the implementation of the one-party system represents a meal ticket for life. But there are many hungry rivals and not just those outside government. The political instability that characterizes African societies is the inevitable consequence.

The military are in a unique position to enter the political free-for-all. The concentrated power of the state machine is focused in the force of arms. The military's access to weapons of coercion provides them with a strong claim to power and influence. Inept governments are all too aware of the military option waiting at the sidelines.

Whatever happens, the bureaucracy carries on administering the resources of the state. The state bureaucracy is one of the most enduring legacies of the colonial era. Their specialist skills, knowledge and monopoly over communication and information are something that no government can do without. Even in post-Amin Uganda, social disintegration notwithstanding, civil servants still retain a degree of coherent organization.

It is the dual function of the African state as an institution of administration and an arena for sharing out economic resources that accounts for its unresponsiveness to the needs of people. The conflicts that go on inside the state apparatus have little meaning for ordinary people. Whether it is an army general or a new ambitious politician who lines his pocket is a matter of indifference for most people. And, as everyone suspects, it is only a matter of time before the new government turns on the people demanding more taxes and more sacrifices.

Changing the state machine

The African state clearly lacks legitimacy. For most Africans their only link with the state is the bribe they are forced to pay to a corrupt official. Popular hatred for the state is widespread as millions of Africans yearn to rid themselves of the yoke of officialdom. Even in countries like Tanzania, where political leaders have relatively clean hands, the bureaucracy is held in utter contempt. Peasants who beat or kill local *Ujamaa* officials are held in high esteem in the Tanzanian countryside.

It is not surprising that there have been many attempts to rebel against state authority. The most widespread of these attempts have been *coups* carried out by junior or noncommissioned officers such as those in Sierra Leone, Liberia or Ghana. Unlike the military *coups* executed by the generals, the ones implemented by junior officers usually carry the promise of radical change. Yet it is strikingly clear that none of the dozens of *coups* have changed anything.

Even with the best of intentions *coups*, be they military or otherwise, cannot change the state machine. The participants in a coup are by definition a select group of individuals isolated from the people. Without popular mobilization or support, the *coup* leader is inevitably forced to turn to the existing state institutions to administer society. A radical *coup* leader may well shake up the apparatus of the state. But even a shake up of the bureaucracy is no substitute for replacing it. The *coup* leader will find that the state bureaucracy carries on as before and sooner or later he will become its prisoner. So is there a realistic alternative to the existing state machine?

Many of the functions of the existing African state would have to be carried out under any form of political order. Administration, communications and the maintenance of order need to be sustained under every form of government. However, the present African state apparatus is not the only option for administering society.

The state apparatus is not a simple technical institution. Rather it is an institution that represents the interests of a clearly defined social group. In the past the colonial state was the instrument of the imperialist powers. After independence the colonial state was captured by the African ruling class who used it to enforce its interests. It is this character of the African state, as an instrument of ruling class power, that makes it so unresponsive to the needs of society. Indeed, one of the main objectives of the state is to coerce society so that the powerful can continue to enjoy its privileges.

The alternative to the existing state apparatus is one that is based on the interests of those classes—workers and peasants—who represent the vast majority of society. A state apparatus representing such interests will obviously have to adopt forms of organization that are not hostile to, but part of society. Such a state cannot simply administer; it has to also represent the wishes of society.

The new state just like the old will have to administer the resources of society. It will need specialists to run technical services and a bureaucracy to supervise the details of administration. The new state cannot do without a bureaucracy. But a bureaucracy as such need not be a problem. The organized specialist skills of civil servants do not constitute a danger to society. We have to distinguish between bureaucracy as a technical function and as a source of social privilege. It is when bureaucrats acquire special privileges that they acquire independence from society. As a distinct social group they acquire a special outlook and instead of *serving*, they attempt to be the *master* of society.

One way of preventing civil servants from becoming bureaucrats is by limiting their access to material privileges. Civil servants should be rewarded, but their payment should not be far above the national average enjoyed by the rest of society.

One effective antidote to bureaucratization is to limit the centralization of administration. Many of the functions of existing administration could be better carried out regionally and even at the local level. Decentralizing administration limits the scope for the emergence of a powerful bureaucracy. Decentralization also makes civil servants more susceptible to grassroots pressure. Local public employees cannot find refuge behind the technical jargon much loved by bureaucrats; they have to account for actions which are visible to people in their community.

Even a decentralized system of administration cannot be trusted to carry on on its own. To ensure that civil servants are working in harmony with popular objectives, it is essential to establish institutions of mass control. Local committees organized throughout the nation, involving people from all walks of life, need to be organized to scrutinize the activities of state administration. The committees can establish an inspectorate that can keep civil servants on their toes. Individual grievances can be channelled through such an inspectorate and publicized throughout the community. Such inspectorates could play an active role in ensuring that administration is carried out in the public interest. It can also play an investigative role in relation to alleged abuse of power and corruption.

The reorganization of state administration along the lines previously discussed provides the starting point for the exercise of popular power. But to ensure that the state is genuinely accountable to society, it is essential to alter the role of the military and of policing. The new state, like the old, cannot do without the monopoly over the instruments of coercion. Defense has to be maintained and public order enforced.

However, whereas in the past the forces of law and order were designed to dominate, now their role is to serve society. To ensure that the military cease being a law unto themselves, they will have to be deprofessionalized. The military will still need professional training but they will no longer be a select, privileged force cut off from the rest of society.

The defense of society is a matter of direct concern for all able-bodied men and women. It cannot be left to an elite force of specialists. A nationalist militia drawing on our youth provides a guarantee that the use of force must have the consent of the majority. A militia that is based on a people armed and trained in the craft of warfare cannot be used to coerce society. Such a militia will only fight if ordinary people see and understand its necessity.

Arming workers and peasants is not just a narrow military matter. It provides the ultimate guarantee of popular power and control over the state. No wonder that there is nothing that the rich and the privileged hate more than a people that are armed.

An organized national militia provides a direct link between the state machine and society. It makes society identify with their state because for the first time it is *really* their state. Only when such a state is established will it be possible to tackle the many problems facing African society. Its establishment will mean a renaissance in African political life.

IX

On Crime and Punishment

Who are the real criminals? The pimps, gamblers, prostitutes, petty thieves and crooks capture the imagination of the press. . . . It would be wrong to blame them for the antisocial activities which now prevail in our cities

It is Africa's corrupt rulers who are the real hard-core criminal elements in African society. . . . The pursuit of their own narrow self-interests has been carried on at the expense of the whole African society.

It has become fashionable to pontificate about the explosion of crime in the urban centers of Africa. Newspapers run sensational articles about antisocial conduct and warn their readers about the dangers that lurk in the night. Among rich Africans crime is a favorite topic of conversation as they contemptuously dismiss common people as the mob. All this accords well with the instincts of the ruling class. Having presided over the disintegration of African societies, the ruling class tries to pin the blame on criminal elements. In this way, social ills are transformed into the problem of law and order. And inevitably the solution put forward is more policing and more coercion. That is why a substantial portion of each country's annual budget is allocated to the military and police forces.

The criminalization of the oppressed

Africa's crisis is not some simple economic affair. Economic decline has promoted social disintegration. Nothing has been left untouched by this crisis. Even the family, the basic unit of society, has been eroded under the strain of economic collapse.

Agrarian stagnation has destroyed the bonds that formerly provided a degree of stability in the countryside. Unable to produce enough even to sustain life, millions of African farmers and their families have turned into roving beggars. All over the continent, even in areas which have been spared the ravages of famine, millions of people are more or less continuously on the move in search of food, a job or anything to keep body and soul together.

In effect a silent social breakdown has taken place in Africa. The cumulative effects of years of agrarian stagnation and shortage of land have forced many people into a more or less permanent state of migration. In many parts of the African continent, the countryside has become denuded of men who have been forced to migrate in search of new sources of income. In many rural areas, almost 50 percent of the adult male population have left for the cities. The disruption of family life on this scale is one of the immediate consequences of a prolonged period of agrarian stagnation.

Forced to leave the countryside, many are drawn into the cities by the prospect of work. The growth of Africa's cities has been catastrophic. Millions have converged on the cities only to find that urban life has nothing to offer them. Jobs are scarce, housing and social services are nonexistent. Under these circumstances, the cities have become a living hell for their new inhabitants.

How long can this continue? The figures tell a frightening

story. In 1950 only one African city, Cairo, had a population of more than one million. By 1980, the figure had risen to 19 cities with a population of more than one million. And it is expected that by the end of the century there will be more than 60 such cities in Africa! And what happens to the millions of rural people who crowd into them? The mushrooming of squalid shantytowns gives the answer. In Lusaka nearly half the city's population lives in squatter settlements and shantytowns!

For the migrants, bare struggle for survival dominates every aspect of their lives. The majority are unemployed for most of the time. Some are able to find temporary low paid work. Others try to go around offering their services. Many try hawking and trading. For all, life is a dead end with no prospects for a better tomorrow. A permanent state of insecurity reduces millions of people to the basic task of just getting by from one day to the next.

The dispossessed have no life. All their energy is consumed in the struggle to survive. Living in these conditions breeds desperation and bitterness. Is it surprising that so many turn to activities that the authorities deem illegal? What other options are available to a migrant torn away from his family, denied a job or a plot of land to cultivate? In reality the dispossessed are by definition criminals. The very fact that they reside in illegal settlements criminalizes them from the start.

Africa's rulers have ensured, through their inaction, that the rural population turns gradually into a nation of vagabonds. Having destroyed the old social bonds, they are now surprised that many are no longer constrained by past values and social norms. Excluded from gainful economic activity, without any stake in society, life itself has become illegal for the dispossessed. In reality, Africa's rulers have created a situation where the law can have no meaning for millions of Africans.

The real criminals

Who are the real criminals? The pimps, gamblers, prostitutes, petty thieves and crooks capture the imagination of the press. Less space is devoted to those who have swindled millions and have plundered Africa's wealth.

In Africa real crime is a thoroughly respectable activity. Governments monopolize the purchase of cash crops, earning millions for themselves. Official food prices are kept deliberately low and marketing boards often make sure that they keep a substantial proportion of the farmers' earnings. Working hand in hand with private traders, the Kenya Maize Marketing Board made a killing by keeping food off the market at a time of shortages.

Nigeria's oil revenue provided a useful supplement to the income of its rulers. Millions of dollars have mysteriously changed hands without even a murmur from the press. Occasionally—usually in the aftermath of a *coup*—some of the sordid details of the crimes of the previous regime are publicized as if they were a thing of the past.

The African press hardly ever wonders why Africa's leading politicians have managed to stretch their salaries to go so far. It is accepted that political power entitles one to have access to the nation's wealth. Acts of crime in these circles are referred to in the press as "good business" and it would be considered bad taste to cast doubt on the probity of the appropriation of wealth through corruption.

It is Africa's rulers who are the real hard-core criminal element in African society. Their ill-gotten gains are, however, only one side of the story. Their real crime consists of the social catastrophe that they have inflicted on Africa and its people. The pursuit of their own narrow self-interest has been carried on at the expense of the whole of African society. They have turned the countryside into a vast tract of rural wasteland and created a life in hell for the masses in the cities. And they have the gall to turn on their victims in the name of law and order!

What should be done

History cannot be turned back. Africa's social disintegration cannot be ignored when looking for solutions. There can be no change for the better unless the problem of the dispossessed is confronted squarely.

It would be wrong to blame them for the antisocial activities which now prevail in our cities. Nevertheless these activities do constitute a barrier to progressive change. In the first place, the victims of these activities are invariably the poor themselves. Furthermore, the widespread fear and suspicion they generate fragments people and forces them to look for individual solutions to their problems. The dispossessed become paralyzed as a social force and, as individuals, compete against each other in a desperate struggle for the few available crumbs.

The solution to these problems lies not in the sphere of criminology. So long as millions of people are forced to live in the poverty and squalor of the existing circumstances, antisocial activities will continue to thrive. It is the circumstances in which the mass of the people now live that have to be changed in order to solve the problem.

Very few people have chosen to live in the blighted

shantytowns or set out to make careers as petty crooks. For most this is the only alternative offered to them by society. Given the chance of gainful employment, the majority of people would jump at the opportunity. The long-term solution to the problem of crime in Africa is to revive agriculture and to provide employment for those without the means of subsistence. In the cities the criminalization of squatters must cease. Instead of periodic police raids they must be offered the legal right to residence. Security of tenure for the shantytown dwellers would go a long way towards removing one of the most frightening elements of African urban life.

Providing employment through the rehabilitation of agriculture is the obvious cure for many of Africa's most pressing social problems. This is not just a matter of economic reality. Stable employment can provide the foundations for the reconstruction of social life. It is a basic precondition for the revival and development of family life. Through such a process a new community spirit can emerge with its own values and norms. Under such conditions the community can learn to police itself. Individuals live as part of a community that is truly theirs and learn to act according to customs and standards of behavior that make sense of their lives.

Even those hardened by a life of crime on the margins of African society can learn to play a positive role in the life of society. Through practical education people can be shown that antisocial attitudes and behavior can provide no answers to their personal problems. For any party committed to change in Africa, the dispossessed represent a real challenge. By involving them in a struggle for change a great deal can be achieved. So-called hardened criminals can be taught that there is more to be gained through collective effort than through individual action. The fight for change provides a focus where, for the first time, they can take matters into their own hands and recapture their self-respect and the human dignity which has been denied them for so long.

Those whom society labels as criminals today will show, in the course of their taking action to change African society, that they are capable of demonstrating the highest of human virtues. Severe punishment should be reserved for political leaders, bureaucrats and public servants who commit crimes of corruption, theft and so on against the people.

X

Reaching for a New Horizon (Media, Culture and Education)

To take part in the African revolution it is not enough to write a revolutionary song; you must fashion the revolution with the people. And if you fashion it with the people, the songs will come by themselves, and of themselves.

In order to achieve real action, you must be a living part of Africa and of her thought; you must be an element of that popular energy which is entirely called forth for the freeing, the progress and the happiness of Africa. There is no place outside that fight for the artist or for the intellectual who is not himself concerned with and completely at one with the people in the great battle of Africa and of suffering humanity.

—Sekou Toure

A new Africa cannot be built through political action alone. The existing system of education, culture and media stupefies and enslaves African minds. Ignorance and superstition are strong allies of the African establishment. Information and the means of communication are carefully controlled and Africans have to make do with word-of-mouth gossip and rumors. Africa's rulers have encouraged a system of culture which reinforces passivity and ratifies the feeling of powerlessness that afflicts the continent. To combat this devastation of the African spirit, we need to fight for the liberation of our minds and establish a culture of change.

Learning for change

Education is a powerful instrument for instilling in people the conviction that the world is there to be made. In Africa, however, education plays an entirely different role. Education has become a scarce resource which African leaders bestow as a favor to a fortunate few.

Instead of education forging a common bond between people striving for the same destiny, it divides Africans in a desperate scramble for places in schools and institutions of higher education. Thus education is not about learning but about establishing one's status in the social hierarchy. Through the system of education the status of the elite is confirmed and its social superiority is legitimized.

The elite character of African education is manifest in its every aspect. Colonial and Western values retain their influence in the curriculum. Instead of teaching about the African experience, students are encouraged to become familiar with the writing of Voltaire and Shakespeare. At higher levels the system of education is linked to Western institutions and examinations. This is not just a matter of convenience nor simply the result of the impulse of the African establishment to ingratiate itself with its Western masters. Africa's leaders show no inclination about learning from the experience of their own society. Least of all do they want ordinary people to study their circumstances. That would be subversive. The imprisonment of popular writers by African governments for the crime of writing about the situation as it is testifies to this.

The content and structure of the system of education in Africa is designed not to *involve,* but to *exclude.* It puts an intense emphasis on competition so that students learn, not for themselves, but against each other. The substance of the curriculum is itself exclusively based on the concerns of Africa's elite. Such a system rewards those who already have wealth. The virtues demanded of the African student are either subservience or an overdeveloped ego.

The present system of education is a barrier to enlighten-ment and cultural change. For those interested in Africa's progress the question of education demands new solutions. Knowledge can be a powerful weapon for extending people's horizon. Through learning, Africans can become conscious of their circumstances and of the possibilities for change. Real knowledge provides the understanding which unites Africans in a common mission of reclaiming their future.

For education to serve the purpose of the liberation of the intellect it must be taken out of the hands of the elites. Even with the best of intentions a system of education cannot be developed by educators alone. The foundation of education must be built around the experience of Africa's people. It must serve to explain that experience and push Africans towards a growing awareness of their circumstances.

Africa's elite educational institutions are a luxury that the continent can ill afford. Elite schools, such as Achimota in Ghana, King's and Queen's College in Lagos or Alliance High in Nairobi and the many other private institutions ought to be abolished. These institutions are in any case not about education but are designed to structure the career prospects of the elite. As such, they reproduce what is worst about African society and train students in the art of studied contempt and arrogance towards ordinary people.

Free education for all is a right that all Africans must enjoy. Liberal education which encourages speculative thought and the elevation of mental work and the degradation of manual activities is of little use to the new Africa. Education cannot be some innocent private affair. It must be planned and directed in line with the developmental objectives of the African nation. It is only common sense that dictates that education should have a strong technical and vocational dimension. Such a synthesis can create the educated carpenters, educated mechanics and educated agronomists that Africa needs.

Elite education is of use only to a handful of rich people who want to preserve the *status quo*. Mass education on the other hand can unleash the creative energies of millions. Knowledge is a detonator for activating those paralyzed by the fear bred of ignorance. Africa's leaders fear knowledge because it brings people that much closer to the truth. The truth will serve Africa's future well.

The present system of education only strengthens people's passive side. The system we want to build, in contrast, will strive to strengthen people's active side. Real learning is not simply about thinking and reading, it is also about doing. Narrow academicism represents the hoarding of knowledge. It is a knowledge that is untested and without practical consequences.

Humanity has only developed its understanding through work and practical experimentation. We did not begin our history with a theory of fire ready made. Mankind first discovered fire by accident, observed it, learned some of its uses and eventually understood how to create a fire by striking two stones. It was this education that eventually led man to understand the chemical properties involved and thus was born the theory of fire.

It is knowledge that is practical that will yield the most results for Africa. Knowledge that throws light on every aspect of life from health to farming allows individuals to acquire greater control over their situation. And the more Africans control their environment the more conscious they become as well. Practical education abolishes the artificial wall that divides classroom from life, and demystifies the aura that surrounds the acquisition of knowledge.

Instead of hoarding it, the party of change has to popularize the use and examination of knowledge. This need not be postponed to the indefinite future.

The testing of knowledge can be effected in the here and now and used for the social good. At the most basic level those who are already educated can develop their understanding by teaching those less fortunate to read and write. A campaign of literacy turns the former student into an educator and develops the cultural level of society as a whole. That this can be done has been shown in Nicaragua where 15- and 16-year-olds teaching adults to read and write is one of the most exhilarating developments of the new society.

A party of change must itself be society's educator. Every party member must also be a teacher, patiently explaining the problems facing society. The party must engage in the organization of education. It must appeal to the natural curiosity of the people of Africa and encourage its supporters to study and learn. Education must challenge, stimulate and involve. The very act of involvement represents a step in the right direction since it establishes a framework for communication and interaction. Such a framework consolidates people's active side which predisposes them to experimentation and new ideas.

Education which is firmly rooted in the lives of the people of Africa can further develop into more specialist directions. A system of mass education does not mean restricting learning to the basics of life. Precisely because of its mass character, education will be more developed because it is based on a wider range of experiences than in its elitist form. Only such an approach can truly raise standards and the level of popular culture. Every modern society needs specialists. And those students who have shown ability and commitment to learning will be directed towards specialist studies.

However, specialist study and higher learning itself will be harnessed to the overall objective of social transformation. The new Africa will not reward dilettantes and professional students. Nor will it encourage them to retire to life in an ivory tower. Students will be expected to practice their knowledge and involve themselves in the transformation of African societies.

Education is one of the most immediate and tangible remedies we have to Africa's ills. Throughout Africa there is a deep-felt hunger for knowledge. Poor peasants and workers are ready to make sacrifices so that their children can benefit from a few years of school. In most African nations, the announcement of the school examination results has almost the character of a national celebration. The desire for learning is there. All that is needed is the will to act. One of the major tragedies of Africa is that its leaders have corrupted education—turned it into an empty status symbol of the elite.

Media for Africa

The mass media has enormous potential for promoting national culture, stimulating our intellect and teaching us about the world. The media cuts across time and space and brings people together through developing a common awareness of what exists.

Unfortunately Africa's media plays no positive role. Africa's newspapers, radio and television are owned by the rich and cater to a small select elite. In the existing circumstances most Africans have no access to any section of the media. Even the price of a newspaper is beyond the means of many Africans.

In many respects it is no bad thing that Africa's media have such a restricted audience. The media are the craven tools of the establishment. They provide no information that is relevant to the lives of ordinary people. They act as public relations agencies for the elite. Instead of extending people's horizons, the media divert attention towards the banal and trivial. Newspapers especially devote their energy towards flattering prominent personalities and leading politicians of the day. Life in the media is one endless story of public receptions, fundraising dinners, combined with sensationalized accounts of local crimes.

There have been many complaints about press censorship and the absence of freedom of expression for the media. The lack of press freedom cannot be denied. But even when one considers that most Africans have no access to the media in any case, the issue of press freedom becomes a secondary one.

The answer lies not in making the existing media more free, but in changing the character of the media altogether. At present the media combines the roles of harmless diversion and elite control. Our objective is to found a media that can mobilize and galvanize the masses.

Creating a relevant African media is part and parcel of a campaign to educate society. The media is not a substitute but an essential element of this campaign. Mass communication can link people together through centralizing information and essential ideas. Used properly, the media can provide the infrastructure around which a campaign of education can be organized.

The media we need must be inexpensive and simple. That is the precondition for making it available to everyone in society. With recent technological developments it is possible to produce equipment (radio and television) cheaply. Through efficient organization even the most far-flung villages can be reached.

The distribution of media resources should be done on a communal basis. They should be a community resource around which education, discussions and entertainment can be organized. At present, the media fragment and isolate those who consume them. The new African media should not be for private consumption but for collective enlightenment. To realize their potential, the media should not just be watched, read or listened to. They should be discussed through an organized framework of community education. Instead of passive acceptance, a two-way relationship should be established between the people and the media. In this way people's impressions, concerns and criticisms can constitute a steady source of inspiration for the media itself. What better way of educating the educators!

Used in this way, the media can harness the energy of the people and provide the framework for the development of popular culture. It would reverse the relation that exists between media and society. Instead of reflecting life at the top, it would synthesize the cultural strands of everyday life and recreate it in an idiom that is at once universal and direct. The media would become communicators in the real sense of the term because now they would really have something to communicate.

Those who argue for the freedom of the press live in another world. What can this freedom mean when the media are denied to the majority? Freedom to say what and to whom? The challenge to communicators and educators lies in establishing a creative relationship between people and the media. Without this relationship Africa's media will continue to have little relevance to the lives of its people.

Cultural renewal

Africa's rich cultural heritage and vitality are negated by its elitist system of education and media. The African establishment makes a big play of the culture of the past, precisely because it is old and therefore safe. It is totally opposed to cultural developments in the present. Why? Because any cultural development that draws on popular emotion and sentiment would necessarily denounce life as it is now in Africa. That is why it is not safe to be a creative writer or artist in Africa.

Most concerned authors and artists are aware of the need to reorient cultural work in a more effective direction. It is all too evident that cultural affairs in Africa are dominated by the state and are indirectly influenced by Western standards and conventions. Unfortunately, without a long term strategy for cultural renewal, the chances of effectively challenging vested interests are remote.

Cultural workers opposed to the status quo often fight as isolated individuals. As individuals, cultural workers even with the best of intentions can easily lose their way. Such dangers are readily apparent in the sphere of African literature, where the critical spirit is in danger of self-destruction. Too often authors and critics who react against the emphasis of state-sponsored cultural life end up retreating into the past. Even the more radical writers and critics remain its prisoners. Today we see the rerun of many of the debates on African culture that took place in the sixties. Questions about what constitutes an "authentic African literature" are still being debated more than three decades after they were first discussed. Is it not a little indulgent in the eighties to discuss whether African literature is restricted to only works written in an African language? What can be gained from a discussion that contrasts African authors writing in French or English with those working in indigenous languages? Surely whether a piece of literature is African is decided not by a literary convention but by society itself. Through its reaction, society acts as a final arbiter of the relevance of a particular example of literary production.

That the issue of what constitutes African literature can still be a matter of debate is symptomatic of the crisis of identity of the African intellectual. So much of the discussion on literature is concerned with emphasizing its Africanness that one cannot help but conclude that its main motivating force is the insecurity of its participants. The assertion of African culture and history was necessary to expose the false claims of Western culture. It was important to emphasize that Africa's identity was to be based on the African experience itself, in order to reject the Eurocentric conventions of Western culture. This assertion of African culture in the sixties was necessary, but simply to cover the ground again in the eighties risks becoming a caricature.

One of the most worrying trends in African literature is an obsessive nostalgia for the past which is usually justified as the retrieval of historical identity. Under the guise of consolidating Africa's cultural legacy, there is a continuous search to find the present in the past. No society can afford to forget its history and cultural heritage, but a society that looks for inspiration mainly in the past risks becoming backward looking. In the case of the intellectuals, a false sense of security gained through finding an identity through history can serve as a substitute for confronting the problems of contemporary Africa.

The celebration of the past is evident in recent discussions on oral literature or "orature." Orature is an important and legitimate component of African culture. Unfortunately, it is promoted not because of its contemporary relevance but because of its significance in the past. The cultural heritage of the past does not provide a ready-made solution to the present. For whatever the cultural idiom, it is the experience of today's society that requires portrayal.

The elevation of traditional African thought and imagination cannot in any way serve as an effective alternative to the predatory Western cultural influences. The battlefield is today's society and today's consciousness.

This is particularly the case with language. Instead of worrying over whether to use indigenous or European languages, African writers ought to devote their energies to decolonizing the conventional vocabulary. Through cultural work, language can be appropriated for the people and the vocabulary can be demystified. The counterposition of indigenous versus European language ignores the fundamental problem that the people of Africa need a language that is national and truly their own.

A popular African culture requires not only the decolonization of language, but the redirection of cultural work towards the masses. It is only through the redirection of this work towards the spiritual and aesthetic concerns of everyday life that an audience can be created for popular culture. If writers and artists want to go beyond the confines of an elite audience they have to adopt a form that is accessible, direct and clear. Such an approach cannot rely simply on artistic skill; it demands a process of interaction with an evolving audience. Artists who are involved by definition need to involve people in their work. Culture production becomes too exclusive if it simply depends on the creativity of intellectuals. It is the job of cultural workers to encourage the creativity of the masses—to help people enhance their power of expression and perception.

A strategy for cultural work requires a comprehensive program of activities. It requires teams of cultural workers ready to engage local communities in discussion and exploration of the problems of everyday life. Local cultural associations and workshops can provide a framework for harnessing the creative urges of people, and training and educating the community. Mobile libraries, movie projection teams and travelling artists can provide a constant stimulus for enriching the spiritual life of the local communities. They can provide an ever increasing participation of a new audience and thus help establish a secure foundation for popular culture.

Initiatives in the sphere of culture provide one of the most effective means of tapping the potential for creativity and social change. The stakes are high. A revolution in culture is one of the strongest forces for the liberation of the mind. New images, a new language and new symbols will also bring a new audience with a new outlook. Out of such changes will be born the New Africa.

XI

On the African Intellectual

In the modern world technical education, strictly tied to even the most primitive and unqualified industrial work, must form the basis for the new type of intellectual.

The mode of existence of the new intellectual can no longer consist of eloquence, the external and momentary arousing of sentiments and passions, but must consist of being actively involved in practical life, as a builder [and] organizer.

—Antonio Gramsci

The African intellectual has valuable skills, special responsibilities and a lot to answer for. Reading, writing and scientific knowledge are essential to the propagation of new ideas. African intellectuals could play an enormously valuable role in constructing the new Africa.

Unfortunately the African intellectual has lost his way. This is not surprising since more than any other section of African society, the intellectual is the product of Western institutions and ideals. Universities reflect standards and norms which have very little to do with Africa. Even when efforts are made to inject material into the curriculum that is relevant to Africa the results are disappointing. It is the appropriation of foreign models of learning that is responsible for the creation of an intellectual who is not quite at home in Africa.

As products of Western inspired institutions, intellectuals always had an ambiguous relationship to African society. During the colonial era this ambiguity was resolved in favor of participating in the movement for independence. Many intellectuals played a positive role in promoting the cause of freedom. And for the first time intellectuals found their place in society. Once independence was achieved the unresolved tension between the Western trained intelligentsia and African society came to the surface. Occupying a distinct social space, even radical intellectuals have found it difficult to relate to the preoccupations of ordinary people.

African intellectuals cannot be blamed for their tenuous link with society. They are products of forces beyond their control. As such it is more accurate to characterize them as intellectuals who live in Africa than as African intellectuals. While their dilemma is entirely understandable, they should be held to account for the lack of progress that intellectuals have made to Africanize themselves. To avoid misunderstanding it is necessary to state that by Africanization we do not mean a narrow obsession with African themes. Rather the emphasis must be on developing an organic relationship with the people of Africa. Only in this way can intellectual work embody the shared experience of society.

The strategy of establishing African departments at universities has been a step in the right direction but has done nothing to transform the role of the intellectual. The problem of the intellectual cannot be reduced to the subject matter pursued. It is entirely a question of the relationship between intellectual and society. There is no intellectual solution to the problem of the intellectual—the answer lies in changing the social position of the intellectual.

To this day intellectual work is assessed on the basis of criteria derived from the Western university system. The ultimate recognition of intellectual work comes from abroad and as a result research and writing is externally directed. Western authorities continue to pass judgement and their publishing houses have a near monopoly on the African market. The direction of intellectual work is towards an audience other than that of African society. There are too many who wholeheartedly accept this state of affairs. Thus intellectuals look forward to the next international conference and would rather discuss with Western academics than enter into a dialogue with their own people.

Without the direct pressure of social forces many intellectuals go stale and complacent. Too many are happy to live off the glory of their PhD's and cease their research altogether. Others reconcile themselves to a routine of going through the motions and play no role in the investigation of the problems facing their society. Even the basic textbooks designed for African students continue to be authored by Western specialists. Some intellectuals are beyond redemption. They have used their training and education for the sole cause of self-advancement. Many have prospered in business and politics or as apologists for the existing political order. Fortunately, not all intellectuals have followed the self-seeking path. Many are intensely conscious of the unsatisfactory position of the intellectual in Africa. Those who are aware of their responsibilities to society have an important role in the construction of a new Africa.

The evasions

However, at present the African intelligentsia has retreated to the sidelines. They have developed special skills as observers, voyeurs and commentators. The virtues which are prized most highly among our intelligentsia are those of introspection, cynicism and self-celebration. It is almost as if the African intellectual has opted for permanent exile. In many cases the African intellectual has chosen exile in a direct sense. The brain drain to the West is one feature of the corruption of African intellectual life. But those who remain in Africa lead a life of voluntary internal exile isolated from society. It is necessary to reverse this trend and intellectuals must immerse themselves in their society and learn from the masses.

It is commonplace for the African intellectual to blame everyone—governments, generals, the apathetic masses— everyone, that is, except himself. The African intellectual has made a virtue of his own powerlessness. "What can we do?" "How can they understand us?" are some of the questions posed in defense of inaction. In the meantime the African intellectual is happy to receive the crumbs from the table of his master. The more daring will on occasion take the liberty of passing a sarcastic remark about the philistinism of the government. Among the intelligentsia such deeds are taken to be acts of exceptional courage.

It is too easy to blame cynicism on the bad times that prevail in Africa. It is not hard time that breed cynicism. Such historic periods can also provoke resistance and clarity. Cynicism is the product of isolation—in this case self- imposed—and the abandonment of the search for solutions. In Africa, cynicism legitimizes the passivity of the intelligentsia and at the same time discredits all attempts at purposeful change as hopelessly naive. This attitude is a barrier to be overcome.

In the sphere of intellectual endeavor the evasions are striking. The African intellectual has learned to avoid the present and has his eyes fixed firmly on the past. It is now quite fashionable to argue that socialism and capitalism are

alien imports and that Africa has its own model of development.
When pressed to explain, the answer becomes incoherent,
almost mystical. Inevitably the arguments about the African
soul, Negritude or African humanism turn on retrieving some
distant golden age.

Unfortunately, the answers to Africa's problems do not lie
in the past. African unity cannot be realized through a
mysterious substance which worked in the past, then was lost
for a century, and now waits to be rediscovered by a clever
philosopher. It is one thing to use the past for inspiring us in
the present. It is quite another to seek refuge in another era so
as to avoid the complications of the present. In this instance
looking back means giving up on the future.

Without a doubt Africa does not need foreign models. But
those who argue that Africa is exempted from capitalism or
socialism become apologists for the *status quo*. For what
exists at present throughout the continent is the capitalist
market. And what about socialism? It is possible to quibble
about words but in Africa like anywhere else the first step
towards socialism is the removal of this market.

For now we are far from insisting that the African
intellectual accepts our vision for social change. What we ask
is for something simpler—a commitment to change. Africa
needs an intelligentsia that is fully involved in society. Not
everyone can make this transition. Those bloated from too
much beer and too much self-indulgence will find commitment a
threat; an annihilation of the comfortable sanctuary. But
those who are prepared to act will find the experience a
rewarding one. The destruction of self-imposed exile will
bring the African intellectual closer to ordinary people and
provide him with experiences necessary for the emergence of
a new dynamic intellectual climate.

Intellectuals, whether they like it or not, are still part of this
world. Like everyone else they have to make choices and take

sides. University qualifications do not absolve intellectuals from taking a stand. The refusal to do so has no virtue—it is a symptom of moral cowardice. It is cowardice to plead special dispensation on the ground that the problem is "complex" and the choices not entirely to one's liking. Inaction is itself a choice—moreover it is nothing less than opting for the *status quo*. Intellectuals who refuse to get involved are rejecting experimentation; an attitude unworthy of the term "intellectual." By contrast, involvement in the struggle for a new Africa can only redeem the intellectual. It represents the transformation of an irrelevant observer into an active contributor to social development.

Changing attitudes is the point of departure. But to be of relevance intellectuals must change the way they work. The ivory tower ambience is suitable only for those who seek refuge from life. It acts as a positive hindrance for those who seek to create a relevant intellectual climate. In an ivory tower institution the object of inquiry is necessarily arbitrary. Research is a matter of chance or individual choice. It is only when intellectuals learn to test their knowledge in the school of everyday life that they can become aware of what problems society requires them to discuss and solve.

The widely held view which equates intellectual work with academicism bears little relation to the African reality. The challenge of producing relevant new knowledge obliges real intellectuals to expose themselves to the practical issues facing society. Who else is to produce this knowledge? The special training and expertise of the intellectual places him in a key role in the struggle for a new Africa. We have every right to demand that this training becomes the property of society and ceases to be wasted inside an exclusive club. To them we say, "Come home and help forge the identity of the African intellectual."

XII

For the Emancipation of African Women

The emancipation of women is not an act of charity, the result of humanitarian or compassionate attitudes; the liberation of women is a fundamental necessity for change, the guarantee of its continuity and the precondition for its victory. The main objective of any meaningful change is the destruction of the system of exploitation and the building of a new society which releases the potentialities of human beings, reconciling with labor and nature. This is the context within which the question of women's emancipation arises.

—Frelimo

The inferior social status of women in Africa is a permanent indictment of the lack of leadership and of the lack of vision that haunts Africa. Women have been excluded from playing an active role in the continent's social and political life. Worse still, Africa's crisis has had a disproportionate impact on the everyday life of women. More than any section of society, women have had to pay the price of the collapse of African leadership.

Unending work

The traditional role of African women as mother and housekeeper is publicly recognized. What is often ignored is that women not only look after the home but also do most of the work in agriculture. Africa's farmers are mainly women.

Throughout Africa it is women who till the land, travel to the market and carry the heavy loads associated with agricultural work. The burden that falls on women has increased in recent decades. With the ever increasing migration of men from the farms, women have been forced to assume new responsibilities in the countryside. As men leave for the cities, women are forced to carry on working harder and more intensively than ever before.

The extension of women's economic responsibilities in the countryside has not been matched by a growth in power and influence. Indeed, there has been a deterioration in the social position of women. During the past two decades there has been a shift in political influence towards the cities. Africa's power relations have marginalized the rural areas and the women who farm the land.

Even in the countryside itself there has been a decline in the position of women. In the past, women seldom owned land but at least they had closely defined rights to *land use*. These rights allowed women access to land even after the death of their husbands. In recent decades these rights have been eroded by the extension of cash crop farming and the growing importance of the market in land. This escalating value of land has encouraged the single ownership of land at the expense of women. Women's land rights have increasingly come under threat as men have taken direct control over the available land. As a result, women are now less independent economically than in the past.

The stagnation of agriculture and the general impoverishment of the countryside has intensified women's work. The elementary struggle for survival now requires more effort and work. Soil erosion often means that women have to work harder and travel farther to grow food for their family. Declining water resources and the disappearance of trees for firewood force women to walk farther for the essentials of life. According to one estimate, women in northern Ghana require a whole day to collect three days' supply of fuel wood. In rural Kenya, some women may spend 20-24 hours per week to collect firewood. The common sight of women with babies on their backs carrying large loads testifies to the immense contribution they make to sustain life in the countryside.

Men can migrate. But for women there is little escape. The only prospect for women is never ending work at home and in the field. Those women that end up in the cities soon discover that there is even less for them than their menfolk. That prostitution is often the only alternative available to women shows just how far Africa is prepared to degrade its mothers and sisters.

Breakdown of the family

Africa's social crisis cannot but leave its imprint on the family. With so much uncertainty and insecurity the family acquires a special importance as a haven from the pressures of life. Through migration families are broken up, separating husband and wife.

The new pressures on the family are above all experienced by women. In many cases women have to accept the entire responsibility of running the family. Women at once have to serve as mothers, nurses, cooks, cleaners and providers of food and clothes. In a very real sense women have become prisoners of a family-system on which the survival of everyone depends. It is ironic that African societies depend on the family as the essential unit of survival while doing everything possible to undermine it. Under these conditions the family is only maintained through exacting a terrible sacrifice from women.

The inferior position of women in society is perpetuated by a system which relegates them to the position of domestic slaves. There are no avenues of escape from this status. Even the very limited openings available to men—education, jobs, the army, etc.—are closed to women. With so little to go around, Africa's governments have reserved scarce resources for men. Not surprisingly, the African establishment is strongly committed to the idea that a woman's place is in the home. With the help of the media, public opinion has been mobilized against those women who strike out on their own in search of a better life.

That such unworthy sentiments against women have a degree of popular resonance is not surprising. For many men who already face a world without a future, women who join the labor market are often perceived as a potential threat. Brutalized by a desperate struggle for survival, men are often led to take out their frustration on those who are in an even more vulnerable position.

The African condition conspires to exclude women from social life. Outside of the drudgery of domestic work, society has little to offer women. Women face discrimination from cradle to grave. Even the limited education extended to women is looked upon as a favor rather than as a right.

Of course not all women are excluded from access to higher education, wealth and prestige. The wives, daughters and mistresses of Africa's elite are treated politely and with respect. The African establishment makes sure that its women escape the indignities suffered by the rest of the female population. Once in a while a woman is chosen as an ambassador or junior minister to symbolize the enlightenment of the elite. Of course, there are the official women's leaders. Carefully cultivated elite women are promoted as the voice of society's women.

These official women's leaders rarely come into their own at the many stage-managed conferences that Africa's politicians love so much. Here women leaders deliver the predictable speeches on the values of motherhood, health and education. Organizing charities is their main activity. In between conferences and charity events the official women leaders disappear and resume their role as wives, daughters or mistresses of politicians and businessmen.

Unfortunately the African feminist movement serves as the mirror image of the official women's institutions. More often than not what separates the two is a gap in generation. The feminists are younger but in every other respect share the mood and lifestyle of their elders. That African feminists are urban based, academics, professionals and isolated from the rest of society shows its limitations. However, no one's social origins can be held against them. The real problem of African feminism is not its social origins but its social concerns.

African feminists remain trapped within the preoccupations of their own narrow and ultimately elitist environment. Their quest is for their equality within the elite rather than the liberation of the mass of women. The day-to-day degradation of ordinary African women is an experience that feminists look upon from the viewpoint of a charity worker or a missionary. This is not surprising since their social position makes them ill-disposed to empathize with the lives of ordinary working women. As a result, the issue of women has been narrowed down to the specific objectives of advancing the status of a select group of privileged females.

Feminism as it now exists is simply a second-hand version of its Western equivalent. The struggle for women's liberation cannot begin at the top—it must address the specific forms of oppression experienced by women in Africa. Such an approach cannot restrict its perspective to the immediate problems of women since female oppression is reproduced through the complex of institutions that are destroying Africa as a whole. A precondition for sexual equality is the establishment of social and economic independence for women. That's why the consistent pursuit of women's liberation requires the perspective of broad radical social change.

What must be done

It is inconceivable that Africa can be transformed without altering the position of its women. How far can African societies go without the participation of over half the population? For those Africans who want to build a new world, fighting for the emancipation of women is not an option. Nor is it some favor extended to women. Africa needs the energy, enthusiasm and commitment of its women if it is to break out of the present impasse. Nor should anyone forget that of all sections of society, women have the most to gain and the least to lose from progressive change.

In the past, particularly during the anti-colonial struggle, women have shown the important role that they can play in the fight for change. Today, in South Africa, women stand shoulder to shoulder with men in the violent confrontation against *apartheid*. This is the example that should inspire the new leaders of Africa.

A party of change cannot simply fight for women's rights as part of a general package of demands. The experience of women's oppression takes on special forms which must be addressed in specific ways. It requires special forms of organization that take into account the disadvantages suffered by women and act as a bridge to bring them into active social and political life. The party of change must set about creating mass organizations for women and train specialists to conduct this important sphere of political work.

A party of change must set about fighting every obstacle that stands in the way of women playing a full and equal role in every aspect of social life. All backward prejudices which insult and degrade women must be fought. The view which portrays woman as the mere appendage of man acts as a barrier to real emancipation. Every form of discrimination—be it economic or educational—must be confronted if women are to acquire the independence that is essential for their participation in social and political affairs.

The fight for women's rights cannot be postponed to the indefinite future. A party of change can make a major contribution by establishing the correct standards for dealing with women. It can set an example by not marginalizing the question of women or allowing it to become the monopoly of a handful of specialists. Instead the party, through its actions, can place the issue of women, as a matter of concern, in front of all Africans where it truly belongs.

New political attitudes must necessarily reflect a new approach towards the position of women. The party can't simply talk about the question of women; it must show, through its own actions, that it is prepared to take the lead. Inside the party every opportunity should be taken to involve women in its activities. Party members must set a personal example and backward, anti-women views must be confronted, exposed and isolated. If this battle is consistently waged then a climate which is hospitable to women will be established.

One of the real tests of the party's effectiveness in fighting for the rights of women is its ability to train and promote women leaders. It must set out to establish not token, but real women leaders.

There can be no justification for excluding women from leadership. Women leaders are the clearest guarantee of equal access to power. A party led by women and men can serve to anticipate the society of the future. Africa will be twice the stronger for that!

XIII

The Dream of African Unity

> *... Africa's freedom will only come through united action. The unity has to come before there will be any great advance against the remaining bastions of privilege and racism. And the unity can be strengthened by many different methods; by economic co-operation, by improved communications, by political unions, and so on. Any step to unity is a help provided that the ultimate goal of a united Africa is not precluded. And every step forward can have intermediate effects of strengthening the freedom fight, and also strengthening our powers of resistance against the pressures of international imperialisms. But we must never lose sight of the ultimate goal, nor mistake interim steps for the achievement.*
>
> —Julius Nyerere

The July 1985 conference of the Organization of African Unity (OAU) was a sad affair. Meeting in the capital of poverty-stricken Ethiopia, the African leaders thanked Western donors for the food they received while pleading for some relief from the onerous conditions imposed on the continent by the International Monetary Fund (IMF). An organization purporting to represent African unity had become an institution of supplicants.

111

Everyone knows that the OAU has become an empty shell—at best a talking-shop designed to boost the reputations of unpopular politicians. The OAU has no power or legitimacy. It has done nothing to promote African unity. Perhaps its only role is to be a clearinghouse for Western debt collectors.

From a dream to a nightmare

There was a time when the goal of African unity really meant something. The development of the anti-colonial struggle throughout the continent led to a growing awareness of the African condition. For many activists the struggle against colonialism showed that the salvation of all Africans was inextricably linked. Against the powerful colonial masters only a continent-wide solution could work.

The prime mover behind the establishment of an organization of African unity was Kwame Nkrumah. Nkrumah convened two conferences in 1957 and 1958 with a view to establishing a center for coordinating the struggle for liberation throughout Africa. The All-African People's Conference was the first serious attempt to give an organizational expression to the dream of African unity.

But there were strong forces at work determined to wreck the movement for unity. The colonial powers had most to lose from a united Africa. They therefore set about provoking regional rivalries. Many African leaders who remained dependent on the old colonial masters followed suit. Between 1958 and 1962 a series of regional blocs emerged throughout the continent. Africa became divided on the eve of its independence.

It was these regional blocs that were to serve as the foundation of what was later to be known as the OAU. The

OAU established at a conference of African nations at Addis Ababa in May 1963 represented a compromise. It established an organization which accepted the reality of a divided Africa and reduced the meaning of unity to empty rhetoric. Thus, a "division of labor" was established: African nations would continue to promote their narrow objectives, often at each other's expense, and the OAU would attempt to regulate the rivalries.

It was a tragedy of historic proportions that even committed Pan-Africanists accepted the OAU compromise. A united Africa, asserting its independent interests, promoting the cause of liberation, would have made all the difference in the subsequent decades. Instead, diplomatic expediency prevailed. Some agreed that the OAU was better than nothing—at least a step in the right direction. Such justifications for the compromise were very much misplaced. Every year Africa became more and more divided. As one regional war after another broke out the idea of African unity became more and more discredited. For most people the irrelevance of the OAU served as proof that African unity was unrealistic rather than seeing that this compromise never gave unity a chance to work.

Africa has paid a high price for the absence of unity. Rivalries among African nations, often leading to wars, have led to tremendous destruction. Outsiders have stepped in to take advantage of the conflicts and the break up of Africa is not a prospect that can be discounted.

Arguments for change

If African unity is simply an unrealizable dream then the continent has no future. On their own, isolated from each other, the 45 countries of sub-Saharan Africa cannot develop as independent units. Africa is simply too fragmented to develop its skills and resources. A pragmatic division of labor established on a continental foundation would ensure an efficient use of resources and ultimately economic independence.

As matters stand, Africa's fragmentation serves only the interests of foreign powers. Most African countries have closer economic and political links with outside nations than with each other. This is not surprising since on their own Africa's nations cannot sustain their independence.

Since the sixties the growth of political divisions within Africa has been paralleled by an erosion of its independence. With the passing of time African countries have loosened their links with each other and strengthened the chains that tie them to their old colonial masters. African countries are only independent against each other: as against foreign powers, they remain all too dependent.

Most of the former French colonies in Africa remain an integral part of the old empire. There are 470,000 expatriate French in West Africa. This is ten times more than the number of French expatriates living in the colonies at the time of the granting of independence. An astounding 30 percent of the top civil servants in these countries are French. It is a legitimate question to ask: "Who runs these countries?"

The old French colonies are only a more extreme example of the general pattern. British economic influence in Kenya, Zambia or Zimbabwe is dominant. Belgium and France run Zaire. Instead of uniting against foreign economic influence, African countries are fighting each other for favors from the West.

Western domination of Africa is by no means merely an economic affair. There are 10,000 Western troops in Africa—

the vast majority of them French. Other countries prefer to adopt a lower profile. Britain has "military advisers" in Ghana, Nigeria, Sudan, Swaziland, Uganda and Zimbabwe. It maintains overflying, training and defense agreements with Kenya. Belgium has a military cooperation agreement with Zaire. And the United States has set up key operational bases in Somalia and Kenya.

More importantly, the influence of Western powers in Africa is growing all the time. While French paratroopers battle on in Chad at one end of the continent, South African troops walk about freely in Botswana at the other end. Even countries that in the past have attempted to stand up to foreign interference have caved in. Sekou Toure, leader of the anti-colonial movement in Guinea, refused to compromise his country's independence with the French authorities. But, by the time Sekou Toure died in 1984, the French were back and the Israelis were in the wings waiting to sign a diplomatic agreement.

The growth of foreign political influence is a matter of life or death for Africa. A divided continent will become a hunting ground for foreign adventurers. And it is only a matter of time before a new "scramble for Africa" begins in earnest. Until now the sordid record of the OAU has shown that Africa is not a master of its own fate. But matters will not end there. Others will move in and strengthen their grip over a divided continent.

Time to change course

African unity is not an optional factor but a prerequisite for the assertion of African independence. The future of every African country depends on resolving this fundamental question. Africa is ignored in international forums and not even consulted about its own affairs. The future of Chad depends on negotiations taking place in Paris. South Africa and Namibia have become international rather than African issues. Africans look on while London, Washington or Paris monopolize the diplomatic initiatives about the future of *apartheid*. Angola has become a pawn in superpower diplomacy. More and more, all the important issues concerning Africa are decided by foreign diplomats.

Where to start? Pan-Africanism is not a well-meaning philosophy but a matter of practical necessity rooted in the conditions of the continent. Progressive change in any African country is intimately linked to the forging of alliances with the forces of change throughout the continent. The more Africans learn to work together and rely on each other, the less they will be prey to foreign domination.

African unity cannot be left to the niceties of diplomatic protocol. It is not some ideal that can be declared, signed and delivered by a handful of diplomats. It has to be developed through involvement and the common experience of struggle. If unity is simply portrayed as a worthwhile ideal, without practical consequences, it will have no meaning for the people of Africa. Unity will only acquire coherence through confronting practical issues from a Pan-African point of view.

It is as well to start with South Africa. The struggle against apartheid is in the interest of every African. At present it is the black South Africans who are in the firing line. However, the Pretoria regime represents a threat to every part of Africa. The people of Angola, Botswana, Mozambique and Namibia know only too well what to expect from South Africa. Until apartheid is destroyed, no African nation can feel at peace. Supporting the struggle against apartheid is not a question of sympathy or altruism towards those who suffer under the yoke of the racist regime—it's in the direct self interest of every African. Establishing a movement of solidarity with the liberation struggle provides a clear focus for the forging of African unity.

A well organized movement directed against apartheid could mobilize the creative energy of Africans throughout the continent. It could provide valuable assistance to the liberation movement and hasten the day of victory. Such a movement could bring together the most energetic and far-sighted activists who are concerned with the failure of African unity and independence. A movement of All-African Progressive Forces (AAPF), built initially around the struggle against apartheid, could provide the wider framework for the assertion of African unity.

It is important to learn the lessons of the past. Unity cannot be sought at any price. Uniting with African puppet regimes is necessarily at the expense of Africa's independence. The experience of the OAU has shown that an institution ostensibly established to promote African unity has become part of the network of Western interests.

Establishing a framework for African unity through the existing governments makes little sense. The existing governments fear real African unity because of the threat it would represent to their divisive policies. African governments are in any case too much influenced by foreign interests to do more than pay lip service to unity.

The movement of AAPF must start from below. It must bring together those forces who are already committed to African unity: liberation movements, progressive political parties, trade unions, women's organizations and so on. It is these forces that will want to fight against apartheid and also to build a new Africa. Through mutual cooperation and work the different constituents of AAPF will derive strength and maximize their impact on society. Even in its early stages the AAPF must act as a forceful pressure group, asserting the interest of Africa over every new development. By its action the AAPF can act as living proof that the ideal of African unity is a realizable objective.

Although the AAPF will have a modest beginning, its objectives are far-reaching. Mobilizing opinion and support for liberation in South Africa is only the first step in drawing out the compelling argument for a real all-African solution to the problems facing society. To win support and build a new consensus the AAPF must seize every opportunity to popularize its objectives. In particular it has a special duty to alert Africans to the danger represented by foreign domination. By exposing the extent of external control the AAPF will be able to argue the advantages of a continent-wide approach with conviction. The program of the AAPF should consist of the following objectives:

1. The liberation of all parts of Africa
2. The withdrawal of all foreign troops from Africa
3. The dismantling of all foreign bases in Africa
4. The cancellation of all foreign debt
5. The establishment of an African Common Market with a view to setting up a secretariat for regulating economic development throughout the continent.

The promotion of these objectives should be pursued from the wider perspective of defending the interest of the whole continent. Africa will stand united, or fall divided! A united Africa can no longer be the hunting ground of foreign adventurers. Its demand for a new economic order will not be ignored. As a united force Africa will have the weight to negotiate the terms of its involvement in the world economy. It can reclaim its resources and assert control over its economic destiny. The irrational national boundaries imposed by the colonial powers which doom countries to economic dependence will be no loss to Africa. It is an Africa that's not of our making. Our objectives are only modest—all we want is Africa.

XIV

Africa and the World

> *There can be no coexistence between independence
> and imperialist and neocolonialist domination; be-
> tween independent Africa and racist, minority, settler
> governments. . . . Until colonialism and imperialism
> in all their various forms and manifestations have
> been completely eradicated from Africa, it would be
> completely inconsistent for the African revolution to
> coexist with imperialism.*
>
> —Kwame Nkrumah

Africa has been ill-served by its leaders. As previous
chapters indicate, Africa's independence has been
mortgaged and the attempt to assert control over the continent's destiny has been abandoned. Africa is less free and
more divided than it was in the sixties. At least then Africans
shared a common dream and a common purpose. The first
generation of leaders have succeeded in destroying that
dream as Africa becomes engulfed by their nightmare.

Africa has no weight on the international scene. Most
African states have turned into the client states of this or that
foreign power. Foreign economic and political interests are
given a latitude to operate in Africa not available anywhere
else in the world. African diplomats do not negotiate. At
international conferences they are treated as equals only

during public engagements. Behind the scene their role is that of supplicants. In turn foreign envoys need not have any headaches about Africa. The maintenance of external interests in Africa can be safely left to the army of charity workers, expatriate experts, businessmen and military advisers who inhabit the continent.

As argued previously, a consistent policy of social transformation and the consolidation of African unity would go a long way towards reversing the balance of power between our continent and that of foreign interests. A new dynamic domestic environment will lead to the surge of confidence that is necessary to reinstate Africa's claim to its own future. But to secure this future Africa needs not only far-sighted national leaders, but also good diplomats. A new diplomatic strategy, one that is at once resolute and pragmatic, is essential if Africa is to assume its rightful place in the international system.

African diplomacy can only succeed if it is able to seize all opportunities available to small states in international relations. Fortunately for Africa the global system is not a monolith. Far from it. Even within the two main superpower alliances there is considerable strain and tension. The international system is governed by a vast array of rules and regulations. This framework helps only to modify the conflict. In everyday international relations the advancement of one country is seen necessarily at another one's expense. Competition within and between power blocs is intense. It creates a much needed space for African countries.

African diplomats must learn to use foreign rivalries to advantage. At present it is the reverse that is in evidence. Foreign powers are able to benefit from the rivalries that inflict our continent. Angola is only the latest hostage to foreign interference generated by indigenous conflict. Every war between African nations, every civil war and even major regional conflicts provide yet another boost to the power of foreign influence. The main beneficiaries of the Somali-Ethiopian war were foreign powers. While conflicts in Chad, Sudan and Uganda have benefited no Africans, they strengthened foreign influence in the area. All this bitter experience ought to teach African diplomats a thing or two.

African diplomacy can benefit enormously from the desperate economic competition that plagues the West. Western countries at the moment take Africa for granted. In particular, Britain and France regard their old colonies as guaranteed markets, sources of raw materials and spheres of investment. It is the job of Africa's diplomats to ensure that no foreign power can take it for granted.

Effective diplomacy is one that takes the long-term view, while flexible and adaptable enough to meet the exigencies of new circumstances. It must be internally coherent but outwardly quite unpredictable. It must combine a ruthless pursuit of African interests with a pragmatic sense of what is possible in a given situation. In the African context, diplomacy must minimize the effects of limited bargaining power and, if possible, turn it into advantage. Our diplomats, like their foreign colleagues, must too learn to make up the rules as they go along, but without ever forgetting that their objective is to defend Africa from the encroachment of foreign interests and to enhance our power and influence.

Diplomacy must not be too secretive. If it becomes a mystified elusive game then African diplomats will find that they will become isolated from their own people. Without active and mass support, African diplomats can have very little in the way of leverage. Diplomatic objectives must be pursued in tandem with the publicly stated goals of government.

A precondition for the effective pursuit of diplomatic

influence is the renouncement of all the old treaties that bind Africa to foreign interests. The renouncement of all the old treaties represents a statement to the world that Africa is reasserting its control over foreign affairs. In proper diplomatic fashion Africa should explain to the nations affected that it is prepared to renegotiate all the old treaties but only on terms which are consistent with the promotion of its own independent interests.

This would give African diplomats a new opportunity to look at the world afresh. It would give Africa new bargaining power. Instead of maintaining close links with one dominant partner, as nations do in Francophone Africa, diplomats could negotiate multilateral deals and agreements. In this way Africa could derive important benefits from international competition. Forcing foreign powers to compete with each other for influence has a double advantage. Through playing off foreign interests none of them will be in a position to exercise predominant influence and, consequently, their overall strength relative to Africa must decline. It is much easier for an African government to deal with five or six foreign nations with limited influence all competing against each other, than one power with an overwhelming political and economic stake in the country. Secondly, dealing with a large number of foreign interests makes economic sense. An African government could use the competing powers to wrest the greatest amount of concessions and get the best possible deal.

African diplomats should evolve a conscious strategy of counteracting the influence of one foreign power by making competing alliances. Political and economic links with the outside world should be carefully regulated. No one interest should have the opportunity to wield influence in key areas. For example, arms purchases should be from several outlets and links should be established with sources of supply from across the board.

One of the biggest dangers facing Africa is the spectre of foreign military intervention. There are already too many foreign troops on our soil. All military assistance treaties should be scrapped once and for all. If Africa tolerates foreign armies to operate inside its boundaries, its diplomatic position is seriously undermined. Foreign bases represent a direct threat to sovereignty and a permanent source of threat to the defense of Africa.

During the past decades African leaders have acquired the unworthy habit of relying on foreign troops to solve internal problems. This indifference to the threat of foreign intervention is explained by the difficulty that many African leaders have in maintaining stability. Often an invitation to foreign armies has been justified on the grounds that it is the only guarantee of national sovereignty. This lame excuse will not do for the future. A nation must fight its own battles. A sovereignty that can only be defended through foreign armies is a sovereignty not worth fighting for.

It is to Angola's credit that it uses foreign Cuban troops not as an alternative, but as a supplement to her army. Angola has faced a bitter and terrible military invasion. Backed by South Africa and other Western interests, rebel forces threaten to destroy Angola's hard-won independence. Angola has received valuable assistance from Cuba. But it has never lost sight of the fundamental point that the war will be won or lost through Angola's efforts.

Outside of the example of Angola, the record of foreign military involvement is a desultory one. African diplomats must not ignore this experience. If military intervention is necessary, then it is up to Africa to rise to the occasion. An all-African army of liberation can serve as the guarantor of stability in areas of tension. The arms and supplies can be purchased from whatever source but the fighting must be carried out by the children of Africa.

A new system of alliances

At present Africa is entwined in a web of alliances which makes no sense for our people. Most are, in effect, imposed on Africa. Since they are negotiated behind closed doors, they are rarely understood by the people concerned. It is only on rare occasions when, for example, South Africa imposed its 'friendship' treaty on Mozambique under the threat of force, that its true content is open to the public view. The existing system of alliances is a huge deception. How can there be an alliance of the exploiter and the exploited? Such alliances as the military cooperation agreement between France and Francophone Africa are nothing more than terms on which foreign domination is to be executed.

Africa needs allies—that is certain. It is in the interest of Africa to win allies who will promote similar objectives in the international arena. But true friends are hard to find. During recent decades it has become all too evident that Africa's friends are few and far between. To restate this simple truth is not to call for pessimism. It is to draw attention to the scale of the task facing African diplomacy. African diplomats must begin from scratch and set about constructing a new system of alliances.

It makes no sense to negotiate alliances with most of Africa's existing diplomatic partners. Most Western countries are only interested in dictating terms. With such nations, relations should be restricted to the economic and sometimes to the cultural sphere. Some European countries, particularly in Scandinavia, have on occasion made an effort to assist our continent. Usually at a price. Handled with care a more comprehensive diplomatic relationship may well be possible with these less predatory Western nations.

The record of the Eastern bloc countries in Africa is a mixed one. The Soviet Union has occasionally supported liberation movements but has always subordinated its assistance to its foreign policy interests. This has had negative consequences particularly in Ethiopia and Somalia. China's record, too, has been similar. African diplomats should pragmatically evaluate their relation with the Eastern bloc. Without entering into any long-term agreements, Africa should enter into temporary alliances with them on specific issues on which both sides have a common agreement. The liberation of South Africa could be one such example— though the Soviet Union's cooperation with Pretoria over the marketing of gold indicates that any alliance would inevitably be a transitory one.

Cuba alone has shown through its spirit of self-sacrifice that it is a worthy ally. Cuba faces many of the problems that confront Africa yet it has been able to show genuine sympathy with the plight of our continent.

Africa and the Non-Aligned Movement

The future of African diplomacy must lie with the non-aligned world. At the moment the nonaligned world exists more on paper than in deed. Nevertheless nonaligned countries of Asia, Africa, Latin America and the Middle East have a profound interest in creating a coherent movement. Organized into one common bloc, the nonaligned nations could exert a powerful influence on world affairs. All nonaligned nations have a vested interest in the recasting of the international economic order. All have a common objective of curbing the influence of the transnational banks and companies that run the affairs of the world economy. It is this common interest that can provide a stable foundation for a new system of alliances for Africa. And it is only with the support of a dynamic nonaligned bloc that African diplomacy will become influential globally.

The nonaligned movement has no alternative but to take itself seriously. It faces a squeeze from the North and has no choice but to look to itself for solution. Recently there has been considerable interest expressed in establishing a permanent international organization for the South. Such an initiative merits serious discussion. It is insufficient to meet periodically in conferences to be worthy of the name of "movement." In traditional parlance that is called a talking-shop. To be effective requires action and action demands organization. World events move fast and will not wait until the nonaligned movement decides to hold its next conference. Unless the nonaligned movement can organize itself to respond to events as they unfold, it can exercise little influence on issues that matter.

The nonaligned movement should take decisive steps towards the establishment of a permanent institution for the South. Africa, in particular, must be active in the creation of such an organization. It could do this by launching a secretariat for the nonaligned movement. Such a secretariat, if it is given serious backing, could act as a permanent influence in international affairs and global economic relations.

At present the South has no institutional framework to discuss its own affairs. The nations of the South are fragmented and take part in regional organizations or institutions like the United Nations and the Commonwealth which are dominated by the North. The North is not inhibited about organizing its own exclusive clubs. Its economic priorities are decided by the OECD and its military ones by NATO. At the United Nations the North simply ratifies the decisions that it has made elsewhere. It meets a fragmented South as a coherent organized force clear about its intentions and determined to pursue them single-mindedly.

Without organization nonalignment becomes no more than an idea. A secretariat could give nonalignment force and influence. Of course it is not realistic to suppose that a secretariat could speak for all nonaligned nations on every issue. Nor can a secretariat encroach on the sovereignty of its constituent members. A secretariat can however acquire real power by coordinating action on those issues on which every nonaligned nation has a common view. It is obvious that an organized consensus on fundamental questions facing the South can make a real difference in international affairs. Even if it does nothing more than make it difficult for the North to divide the nations of the nonaligned world, an important blow for progress would have been struck.

A secretariat of the nonaligned movement could be empowered to coordinate a united response on the following issues:

The Problem of Debt: The nonaligned movement has a common interest in ensuring that the Baker Plan is not implemented. A secretariat could promote a strategy of replacing bilateral negotiations with a united nonaligned strategy. Such a strategy would prevent individual nonaligned nations from being isolated from each other. It could use the threat of cancelling all foreign debt as a lever for getting the best possible deal. If there is no consensus for the cancellation of foreign debts, a secretariat could pursue measures which link interest payments to the price of commodities and thus limit the transfer of resources to the North. A ceiling could be set which would ensure that the service payment on debts is limited to under 10 percent of export earnings.

South-South Economic Cooperation: There is tremendous scope for a renaissance in South-South economic cooperation, as argued in Chapter 5. At present the countries of the North actively discriminate against the poorer regions of the South. Even the newly industrialized countries of Southeast Asia and Latin America face trade restrictions and are actively discouraged from serious involvement in the markets of the North. Commodity-producing Third World countries are facing an orchestrated campaign to keep down the prices of their goods. Indeed one of the sources of economic upswing in the North is the falling price of energy and raw materials.

A secretariat of the nonaligned movement should encourage positive discrimination. This can be most successfully done in the sphere of trade. Preferential treatment for goods from the South could help to establish closer economic relations in the nonaligned world. A step-by-step approach could well begin with preferential trade tariffs and lead to the establishment of a free Southern trading zone. Such a strategy is clearly in the interest of all nonaligned nations—whether industrial or agricultural. Economic cooperation on a world scale also has major political implications. It could help to undermine the strategy of divide and rule which keeps the individual nonaligned nations under the control of Western powers.

Nonaligned politics

Nonalignment must mean more than neutrality. The nonaligned movement has a duty to take a stand against foreign intervention and interference in the Third World. The arrogance of Western powers has been amply demonstrated in recent years in Grenada, Libya and Nicaragua. These examples show that no nation can feel safe and secure from political or military intervention.

As we have argued in an earlier chapter, one of the major targets facing the nonaligned movement is the issue of apartheid in South Africa. It is a sad reflection on the authority of the nonaligned movement that all the major diplomatic initiatives in South Africa are in the hands of international institutions—United Nations, Commonwealth—which are controlled by the North. While the nonaligned world shows only its irrelevance all attention is fixed on the shuttle diplomacy of Western diplomats.

One of the most pressing tasks of a secretariat is the coordination of effective action against the apartheid regime. The concentrated power of the nonaligned movement systematically applied for the cause of liberation in South Africa would signal the arrival of a new force in international affairs. Put another way, more negatively, if the nonaligned movement can play no constructive influence on the future of South Africa it has no right to exist.

AFTERWORD

Bogus Capitalism—
Another False Start in Africa

The IMF programs treat the symptoms rather than the causes. They concentrate on the "money and managerial problems" instead of tackling the structural and external factors that beset Africa's economies. These "reform programs" increasingly being adopted by African governments are designed to make Africa's export producers more competitive with each other. It is a futile exercise, for the more primary commodities the developing world produces, the greater the surplus and the lower the price.

Logically, African nations should be trading with each other and building up a continental network of trade and industry.

History waits for no man or woman. Since this book was finished at the end of 1985, the economic crisis in Africa has—if anything—deepened further. But Africa's reaction to this sad chain of events has remained inchoate and fragmented while the Western-based "development" agencies have taken responsibility for the continent's economic planning.

Such has been the speed of what can be described as the recolonization of Africa by Western bankers and multilateral development agencies that we believe it is necessary to expose the essentially bogus nature of what is being touted as "economic reform" in Africa.

Far from being progressive, these policy changes inflicted on Africa by Western agencies are resulting in the continent's greater dependence on Western finance and economic management. These measures are making worse the already chronic living standards of the mass of African peasants and workers and at the same time intensifying the economic balkanization of Africa.

It is with these concerns in mind that we are presenting this short analysis, as an Afterword, of the implications of these so-called "reform programs" so that African governments can appreciate the dangers of their continued capitulation to these new policy demands.

Africa's crisis has been privatized. A group of well-meaning musicians and athletes have teamed together to raise money to help pull Africa out of the morass. Their generosity and that of the contributors to their aid campaigns are in stark contrast to the official stinginess of both Western and Eastern bloc governments faced with the spectre of widespread famine in Africa.

Of course, Africans must ask the more fundamental question about the crisis—why are we still talking about charity and donors while occupying the most mineral-rich continent in the world? The two are connected—it is precisely because Africa is so rich in minerals that the plunder of the continent and accompanying economic chaos continues today.

What has become clear over the past year is that Africa's crisis is no longer manageable—not for the banks who have financed it, not for the governments who draw their supplies of strategic minerals from the continent, and not for the multinational corporations who have tried to set up a network of profitable manufacturing operations across the map.

Even South Africa, the bastion of white capitalism, is in

economic trouble. The contradictions of a system that keeps 70 percent of its population economically and politically disenfranchized have started to overwhelm it. The rising up of the organized and politicized African working class against apartheid has boxed the white supremacists into a corner. The African working class in South Africa has hardly begun to use its power but already the apartheid regime has blown the whistle and come out in its true fascist and repressive colors.

South Africa is no longer the safe haven for Western capital. In 1985 it announced that it would unilaterally stop its debt service payments. No apologies to red-faced Western bankers, no negotiations, just a politely worded announcement from a Swiss financial adviser that due to its continuing economic crisis South Africa can no longer continue to service debts.

It seems that separate development doesn't stop at South Africa's borders. It's hard to imagine the cries of outrage that would greet a similar announcement from Nigeria, for example reneging on debt commitments. And more to the point, Nigeria—given its present and past style of leadership—would be highly unlikely to make such a radical move.

For as South Africa goes through its political and eventually military contortions, much of the rest of Africa is going through a process of ideological play-acting. Just like the 19th century English monarch who cynically announced to his audience: "We are all socialists now!", African governments are now seeing fit to tell the world: "We are all capitalists now!" Either way the claim is ridiculous.

When the Organization of African Unity (OAU) managed to arrange a special session on Africa at the United Nations early in 1986 it was hailed as a major initiative. They used the session to launch a five year $125 billion recovery plan to which they expected the industrialized countries to contribute one third of the funding. To reassure jumpy investors the recovery plan includes policy recommendations to African governments that are remarkably like those of the IMF and the World Bank.

The plan, which incidentally cost a further $10 million out of Africa's hard-won foreign earnings to formulate, is written in the fashionable jargon of "World Bank-speak" and liberally sprinkled with references to "de-regulation," the need for "realistic exchange rates" and the "dismantling of impediments to the operations of the market." This apparent commitment to the "new capitalism" was loudly applauded by Western representatives at the session. US Secretary of State George Shultz attacked the "now discredited orthodoxies about state-directed development that gave rise to misguided policies that stifle individual initiative." He would replace this, presumably, with a discredited orthodoxy about multinational-directed development that promotes the initiatives of a few individuals on the board of ITT or one of the other multinational corporations that now control about a third of industrial production in the world.

Britain's Foreign Minister, Sir Geoffrey Howe, added his voice to the chorus of approval for Africa's new policy stance. He told African delegates at the UN that they had to recognize "Africa's past mistakes". But he added cheerfully that the development plan was evidence of Africa's new seriousness. The real solution to Africa's problems, Howe concluded, was for "management efficiency to be improved" and for "the restoration of a climate favorable to private investment."

But Howe and Shultz were categorical in their opposition to those elements of the recovery program that would make an immediate difference to Africa's economic plight:

firstly, the demand for international cooperation to establish the means for stabilizing the prices of Africa's primary commodities, and secondly, the call for an international conference on Africa's growing indebtedness.

The link between these two issues is obvious. In 1985 the industrialized countries paid $65 billion less to buy the same quantity of raw materials they had bought in 1984. And the prices of almost all the commodities that the developing world produces—except coffee—are set to decline further in 1986.

African countries are not in a good position to withstand the fluctuations in the commodity markets since they are so dependent on export earnings from one or two commodities. Zambia gets 90 percent of its foreign earnings from copper, Mauritius gets about 90 percent of its earnings from sugar and Gambia gets about 85 percent of its earnings from groundnuts and groundnut oil exports. All these countries are following IMF "reform programs" and all of these countries' economies are chronically dislocated and up to their ears in debt.

And again on the debt question the Western industrialized nations led by America and the UK are fiercely resisting any generalized initiatives on the Third World's or even just Africa's debts. Although an increasing number of bankers have judged substantial sums of Africa's debts to be unpayable, Western governments say they want to deal with debts on a case-by-case basis. This is again so that they can use debt negotiations as another form of leverage to ensure African governments implement the "correct reform policies."

Ironically it is this refusal of the Western industrialized nations to consider the really meaningful reforms—that is, reforms of the world banking system and commodity pricing system—that has currently got Africa by the throat. Until

African countries can guarantee some stability in their income and outgoing patterns, laying any foundation for a self-sustaining and integrated economic development is going to be an uphill battle.

It is the knowledge of this uphill battle that has made an increasing number of African countries opt for the IMF programs and the "new capitalism." Ghana, the Gambia, Sierra Leone, Liberia, Zaire, Zambia and now Tanzania—the list of the countries taking the IMF on board is growing fast enough to prompt one African-owned newspaper to refer to an "IMF triumph in Africa". It was Marx who said that history repeats itself as farce, and it seems that colonialism is repeating itself but this time with smartly suited economists clutching briefcases instead of European soldiers with missionaries bringing up the rear.

The prospects for Africa's "new capitalism" are not good. The IMF's adjustment programs so enthusiastically delivered to Africa's finance ministries place the burden of adjustment on African countries. Although they preach free trade and the unfettered operation of market forces, IMF and World Bank officials have no leverage on the policies of the industrialized countries. So while they are telling African finance ministries to devalue their currencies, slash public spending and reduce their budget deficits, the US is trading with a substantially over-valued dollar and running up the biggest deficit in its history.

The IMF programs treat the symptoms rather than the causes. They concentrate on the "money and managerial problems" instead of tackling the structural and external factors that dog Africa's economies. Currency devaluation—especially in Africa—is seen as the cure-all for economic ill health. But in fact, quick and substantial devaluations do not, in most cases, result in increased export receipts, as inelasticity in demand and supply see to that. But at the same time, devaluations increase the cost of essential imports, causing inflation for which the country's wage earners are rarely properly compensated.

Ultimately the IMF-style recovery programs are flawed by the same problems that beset all externally imposed policies—they can't take into account the realities on the ground in the country where the policies are meant to be implemented. There is a standard IMF program which apparently takes no notice of the different capacities of economies to adjust to external shock.

The reality is that Africa is now a net exporter of capital to the industrialized countries. Bankers estimate sub-Saharan Africa to owe about $125 billion to the industrialized countries, which isn't much compared to the $950 billion which the developing world as a whole is estimated to owe. But the effects on Africa's economies have been severe. In the first five years of the 1980s, Africa's debt service payments have increased from seven percent of its export earnings to a level of 35 percent by 1985.

Under these conditions talk of economic change is meaningless. Any change presupposes the existence of resources which can be more effectively deployed, but Africa doesn't have the capital to develop its potentially rich resources—the small amount of available capital is already claimed by the banks. And in any case, the sort of changes or "reforms" being canvassed by the IMF and the World Bank will do nothing to integrate Africa's domestic economies or to make use of its resources on a continental basis.

These "reform programs" increasingly being adopted by African governments are designed to make Africa's export producers more competitive with each other. But it is a futile exercise, for the more primary commodities the developing world produces, the greater the surplus and the lower the price. And should a developing country successfully produce manufactures, the protectionist lobby in the industrialized countries makes sure these exports are either shut out or priced out through tariff barriers on the market, in the way that the USA has shut out Brazil's steel exports.

Logically, African nations should be trading with each other and building up a continental network of trade and industry. But all the externally imposed "reform programs" ignore this crucial dimension—development is measured by a country's ability to earn US dollars. And in essence the latest waves of "reforms" are more than anything else designed to make Africa safe for foreign investment—the enforcement of an economy directed by a foreign-controlled private sector dictating low wage rates and easy repatriation of dividends and company profits.

Bankers and Western diplomats enthuse about this "new realism" in Africa, but it is in fact just a new desperation. It isn't a new start, it's just a false start down the same road to bogus capitalism.

CONCLUSION

Only the Beginning

*Each generation must, out of relative obscurity,
discover its mission, fulfill it, or betray it.*
—Frantz Fanon

The conclusion to this essay cannot yet be written. We can only state what exists and indicate what ought to be. Everything else is in the hands of the reader and other Africans.

History has not been kind to Africa. Enslaved, partitioned, colonized and then recolonized, Africa has yet to become the master of its destiny. Yet for all that, Africa has developed its own unique culture, spirit and resistance. Everything is there ready to be forged into a powerful movement for change. The era of the movement for national independence and equality has come to an end. With the exception of Southern Africa, formal independence and formal equality have been more or less achieved.

Independence and equality have only exposed the lack of *real* independence and of *social* equality. Independence and equality have represented a mere continuity with the past. The time has now arrived for a major break with the old structures. Freedoms are fine but if they are to mean anything they have to mean freedom from want and material constraint. That is the task of liberation. Liberation or social transforma-

139

tion is the point of departure for real freedom in Africa. There are other alternatives of course. Ethiopia or the grotesque war between Mali and Burkina Faso shows the future of existing trends.

But the alternative can be contemplated only by those who have given up responsibility for Africa's future.

We have no wish to conclude. Our history starts tomorrow or perhaps the day after. It is the struggle for liberation that will close this essay and prepare the way for an entirely new work.

Working Definition of Keywords In Discourse

African political elite: The African political elite encompasses all those who through their access to the state are able to control political life. Because of the relative weakness of the indigenous bourgeoisie, the African political elite has a decisive influence in society. Indeed, access to the state machine is a precondition for the exercise of economic power. The term African political elite comprises a variety of actors—ruling politicians, government officials, top civil servants including the judiciary, military and police.

Barter: Barter implies a form of direct trade without the intervention of money, the market, or the mechanism of credit. It represents an exchange of goods directly rather than through the medium of monetary relations. In the sphere of the world economy, barter can assume the form of *counter-trade* arrangements. Through counter-trade, one country exchanges (not buys or sells) one group of commodities for another group from another country. Through barter and counter-trade, trade relations can be established consciously instead of relying on the anarchy of the market.

Capitalist development: Capitalist development is a form of social organization based on market relations and dominated by the criterion of profit. The creation of wealth is not determined by social need but by the requirements of profit. Such development in Africa has led to a perpetuation of poverty since the utilization of resources has been subordinated to the needs of profit. Capitalist development has failed to develop Africa since, through the medium of the market, the continent's wealth flows continually towards the dominant owners of capital in the West.

Class: A class is a social group with a common relationship to the way that production is organized. In Africa the *capitalist class*, either directly through ownership or indirectly through state controls, owns most forms of wealth. As owners of the means of production and of capital, this class has a common relationship of being exploiters of the labor of others. Large landowners, through the ownership of capital in the form of land, are also a part of this class.

The *working class* is defined by its common relation to the process of production. As a class it owns only its capacity to work. It is forced to sell its labor power and exists entirely on the payment it receives in return. In Africa most of the peasantry can be considered part of the working class. Most peasants cannot subsist entirely on the basis of what they produce on the land and are periodically forced to migrate and sell their labor power. Migrants and the unemployed share with the working class a way of life that depends on the sale of labor power. But in their case, an inability to find buyers for their capacity to work prevents them from having a stable relation with the process of production.

Colonial institutions: Colonial institutions are ones established in Africa by Western powers to enforce their domination over the continent. These institutions are not merely administrative and political. They are also economic—the introduction of the cash-economy, market in land and private property; and they are also cultural—Western oriented religion, education and cultural norms.

Coup d'etat: A forcible seizure of governmental power, usually by military forces. A *coup*, even when led by radical leaders, represents a substitution of a clique for mass action. Hence a *coup* can never bring about social transformation. In general, a *coup* represents merely the expulsion of one group of political leaders from government and their replacement by another.

Decolonization: Decolonization represents the end of Western direct control of Africa. It is the transfer of political power from the European colonial regime to African political leaders. Decolonization results in only the end of *direct* European influence. Often political power becomes formal independence because foreign domination can be exercised *indirectly* through the perpetuation of colonial institutions, e.g., state machinery, civil service and less tangible colonial conventions. If the old colonial power retains its economic influence then political independence acquires a qualified and restricted character. Although decolonization is a necessary step towards freedom, it represents only a step in the process of liberation. (See Liberation)

Dependency: Dependency involves the relationship of the subordination of Africa to the world economy. Dependency theorists often stress the economic inferiority of the ex-colony and its inability to pursue an independent role. In the case of Africa, dependency goes much further. The lack of indigenous economic power makes Africa susceptible to foreign control. Dependence in Africa implies the negation of independence. Hence the recurrence of foreign intervention including the use of military force.

Depoliticization: One of the striking features of post-colonial Africa is the depoliticization of the masses. This process is the consequence of the neutralization of the anti-colonial movement through the monopolization of political influence by the African elite. In the post-colonial era, popular and participatory politics were discouraged as the elite consolidated its power. The marginalization of the mass movement and its failure to realize any of its social objectives have been instrumental in breeding a sense of cynicism and demoralization. A sense of powerlessness born of despair has strengthened the conviction that politics is not for the ordinary man but the exclusive preserve of the elite. It is this mood based on the experience of the dissolution of the anti-colonial movement which acts as a major subjective obstacle to real change.

Development: Development is generally understood as a process synonymous with economic growth. For us, development implies a qualitative transformation of life which cannot be reduced to a series of quantitative indices. Development in the first instance means the growth of society's resources. Through the availability of resources, the quality of life itself changes. As society generates new resources, individuals become less concerned with survival and more with the intellectual, spiritual and cultural dimensions of life. For us, the aim of development is the realization of human potential through the removal of material and social constraint. Economic growth which leaves the quality of life untouched or represents the amelioration of living standards for a small minority is simply growth and does not constitute development.

Ethnicity: Ethnicity is the form of consciousness based on the promotion of ethnic identification. It is an exclusive consciousness which thrives on the elevation of ethnic differences. Ethnicity represents a direct challenge to national consciousness and identity. The concept of *tribalism*, which is often used as an alternative to ethnicity, often conveys a distorted impression. Tribalism implies an organic link with past tradition which is reconstructed as a form of social identity in the contemporary era. In fact, regional rivalries and the exacerbation of ethnic differences are not the residue of the past. They have no organic ties with past traditions but are very much the product of colonialism and the post-colonial era. Ethnicity is not the product of regional consciousness but an outlook encouraged by regional elites. As a force ethnicity is shaped by the conflict of contending regional elites in their striving for political influence.

Feminism: Feminism approaches the issue of women's emancipation from a narrow point of view. It emphasizes sexual differences instead of social ones and hence sees the issue of women as something apart from the wider process of social transformation. In practical terms, African feminists are preoccupied with formal equality instead of social transformation of the position of women. Hence feminism can appeal only to a small circle of privileged urban women. Our critique of feminism is not that it is concerned exclusively with women. Rather, our objection is to the feminist approach which, despite its stated intention, fails to confront the issue of women's liberation.

Ideology: Ideology is a system of ideas that prevails in society and to a considerable extent reflects the outlook of the ruling class. Counterposed to the ruling ideology are counter-ideologies which offer an alternative mode of the world. Oppositional ideas can often acquire force through conveying the mood and aspirations of the population. It is only when the mass movement of working people acquire their own independent ideology that a resolute challenge to the existing order can be said to have been constituted. *Ideological clarity* represents an outlook which is freed from prevailing prejudices and can therefore help people understand that real change *must* and *can* come about.

Imperialism: Imperialism is a concept which explains the general features of a capitalist-dominated world economy. In the era of imperialism, capitalist powers became international powers operating globally. Colonialism and gunboat diplomacy are only an aspect of this striving for international influence. This influence is asserted by economic means through the mechanism of banks and transnational companies. In the case of Africa, often international agencies like the IMF (International Monetary Fund) and the World Bank act as a medium through which imperialist interests are enforced.

Independence: Independence in Africa means the end of direct foreign domination. Independence in Africa has tended to be merely formal as key decisions are often made and generally influenced by foreign interests. Real independence requires not just political but also economic control over natural resources. Otherwise political independence becomes negated by economic domination.

Intellectual: The term 'intellectual' is not used in the conventional sense as someone with formal qualifications and higher education. For us, the African intellectual is one who is able to develop ideas that demystify the prevailing norms and values that obscure existing social relations. Such intellectuals are the product of interaction with the masses. What separates intellectuals from the masses is not their education but their ability to articulate and communicate ideas necessary for the clarification of the tasks facing society. Instead of the intellectual of the ivory tower, the African intellectual is organically linked to the working class.

Leader: The crisis of political leadership is the central concern of this text. Prominent politicians and even heads of state lack the qualities of authority and leadership. In our view, a leader is not necessarily the individual who is placed in a position of power or influence. Most of today's African political elite are officials or administrators. The emergence of African leadership requires individuals who are prepared to earn the right to lead. It is through the struggle to forge a new movement for change that Africa's new leaders will be born. The African leader is thus the product of political engagement and dialogue. Through these means a leadership is constituted—individuals who are truly leaders because as individuals they can now personify the aspirations of the masses.

Liberation: Our usage of the concept liberation is not restricted to its political meaning. In general, liberation is seen to be completed upon the achievement of political independence. For us, liberation requires freedom from economic and foreign domination. But liberation does not merely refer to the material dimensions of life. Real liberation presupposes freedom from prejudice and spiritual and mental enslavement. Liberation is a protracted process through which real freedom is achieved. But it is not a long term objective to be fought for in the indefinite future. Through the liberation struggle in the here and now, the experience of involvement for change helps create the outlook and attitude necessary for the realization of freedom.

Masses: The masses are composed of working people in the urban and rural areas, including the peasantry and the unemployed. It is a political concept that covers all those who have the potential for supporting social change. Those who compose the masses have everything to gain and nothing to lose from such a change. A *mass movement* is one that gives organizational expression to the interests of the masses. It is not separate but part of the masses, and is organized to create a framework for popular participation at all levels of commitment. Thus a *mass movement* is one that is based on *mass involvement*. A mass movement is not distinguished by the number of its members but by its ability to involve and thus ensure that it has an organic link to the local community.

Organization: Organization is often used as a concept signifying a technical or administrative meaning. For us, organization represents a political framework through which political ideas and objectives acquire meaning. Organization brings political philosophers down to earth. It is only when people organize around specific objectives that ideas can be tested, modified and developed. Organization not only gives coherence, but also provides a means through which politics acquires shape and new leaders are created.

Pan-Africanism: Pan-Africanism exists primarily as an elite ideology which sees itself as the relationship of different African nations to each other. For us, Pan-Africanism is not just the sum total of the national components of Africa. Pan-Africanism represents the transcendence of the artificial boundaries established in the colonial era. It is based on the common identity and history of Africa and seeks to forge a united nation on the basis of collective experience. Since most of the problems facing the continent require an all-Africa solution, Pan-Africanism represents a political response to what is in essence the African condition.

Party of change: A party of change is defined by its commitment to transform society through a social revolution. It is a party that is constituted through organizing the masses and through its ability to assimilate the experience of everyday life. Through its organization the party learns from these experiences and itself changes. Only if a party is susceptible to change can it aspire to change society. Thus the relationship between party and masses is one where the interaction transforms both actors.

Political authority: Political authority cannot be attained through a formal title or governmental office. Authority itself is a quality that the masses endow on specific individuals who have earned the right to it. Thus authority can never be imposed from above. It springs from the day-to-day struggles of political life where certain individuals have demonstrated to the masses their foresight, wisdom and commitment to society. Only authority earned through this process gives individuals the *political legitimacy* to be responsible for the running of government. Legitimacy is established through a common identification with the objectives and past record of individual leaders. Legitimacy is enjoyed by political leaders as long as they act in accordance with the aspirations of those who have conferred on them the right to lead.

Political education: Political education is often conceived as indoctrination or the promotion of pure propaganda. For us, political education is a dialogue conducted by activists. The aim is not to put over a line, but to collectively explore the situation facing the masses. Political education does not so much give answers as it raises doubts and questions. Through its encouragement of the spirit of criticism, it creates the basis for mass political action.

Political mobilization: Political mobilization is a term used to characterize the process through which the masses are activated. Mobilization is not simply about winning support for specific action and objectives. Mobilization refers to the activation of political interest and concern. A mobilized mass is the only effective check on the arbitrary use of power.

Mobilization is also the springboard for any political program for action.

Popular culture: A culture is popular if it provides perceptions and ideas in which ordinary people can recognize themselves. Popular culture is based on the experience of everyday life and provides a moral, spiritual and aesthetic idiom for the self-expression of the masses. If it is truly popular, culture will invite involvement and participation. Through its organic link with the masses, it becomes the culture of ordinary people.

Popular leadership: Popular leadership is one that is open to the influence of the masses. It is a form of leadership that is based on *collective* rather than *individual* assertion of influence. Through the process of collective work, a popular leadership learns to lead without losing touch with the grassroots. Its quality of being *popular* is determined by its proximity to grassroots pressure, hence it can remain popular only as long as it is responsive to that pressure and ultimately accountable to the masses. *Popular institutions* are ones through which popular leadership can be exercised. Institutions may be deemed popular if the masses see them as "theirs," if they involve people from all walks of everyday life. Popular institutions provide a basic framework for mass involvement, education and politicization. They provide the means for the elementary expression of the collective experience of the masses.

Realpolitik: *Realpolitik* represents the pursuit of politics exclusively for self-interest and pure power. It is the political culture that dominates the affairs of Africa. Its philosophy is pragmatism and objectives can be established and then changed in accordance with the requirements of the maintenance of political power.

Revolution: Revolution implies a fundamental transformation of society. It is a political act which brings to power not only a new group of individuals but representatives of a new class—in the case of Africa the representatives of the masses. Although revolution is a political act, its real aim is *social transformation.* (See Social transformation)

Socialism: Socialism is a form of social organization which depends on the conscious regulation and distribution of resources. It is based on the elimination of the anarchy of the capitalist market and replaces it with planning. Planning is not a technical device for coordination, but a mechanism through which social priorities can be ascertained and implemented. Socialism recognizes individual differences in talent and skill and rewards people accordingly. But it does not tolerate the right of any individual to exploit another. Socialism seeks to create an egalitarian framework through which social obstacles to individual development are removed.

Social transformation: Social transformation is used to signify the fundamental change of humanly created structures which thwart the potential for development in Africa. Transforming society requires that resources are now put at the disposal of the community instead of private individuals. Through such reorganization, society acquires for the first time conscious control over its own affairs. Such change transforms the most basic relations, conventions and customs. Social transformation is thus the reorganization of society necessary for the realization of liberation. (See Liberation)

The state: The state is an institution through which the dominant interest of the ruling class is enforced. The African state today tends to represent the narrow concerns of the privileged elite. That is why the neocolonial state has such a close affinity with international interests. The persistence of colonial institutions within the African state shows that it stands above and against society. The main objective of the state is to preserve and consolidate the existing socio-economic relations of society. The existing state machinery is not susceptible to reform. Even if the main administrators and civil servants were replaced by those committed to new objectives, the neocolonial state institutions would prove resilient to change. Those who have attempted to use the neo-colonial state for positive ends have become assimilated by the institutions. Thus in Africa it was the radical leaders and not the state that changed. Despite numerous changes in personnel, the state machine has remained intact. The building of a new Africa requires a state that is not owned by the elite but is accountable to the masses. The creation of a new state requires the establishment of a popular counter-institution through which the masses can exert control over their lives. The establishment of local councils, community courts and people's militias are the kind of institutions that can provide the foundations for an alternative source of state power. A new state cannot be created from scratch, it has to evolve through various institutional forms.

Theory of change: To give the yearning for change a real foundation in society requires a theory that can explain why change is not only *possible* but necessary. Such a theory of change cannot be the product of speculation or thought. It can only evolve out of the experience of struggle and from the testing of ideas in day-to-day political life. Through this process ideas acquire shape and problems become clarified. A theory of change provides not only an explanation of society as it really is but also a guide to action.

Third World: Originally, the Third World was used as an apologetic concept designed to promote the idea that the colonial world (of Africa, Asia, the Caribbean, Latin America and the Middle East) was in some sense an equal partner with the rest of the globe. We have retained the usage of this term despite the fact that countries designated as part of the Third World are heterogeneous and live under different social systems and governments. For us, the term "Third World" signifies a common legacy of Western oppression and domination. All Third World countries are poor as a result of colonial and neocolonial exploitation and have faced a continuous threat to their way of life and have had the status of inferiority conferred on them by the world system of imperialism. As a result, to this day Third World countries remain excluded from real influence over the running of the world.

World Order: Based on the international division of labor, the world order is a clearly defined hierarchy of national power. On top are a handful of Western nations and the Soviet Union who determine everything that is important in world affairs. In the middle are smaller industrialized nations. Towards the bottom are the countries of the Third World, and at the very bottom are the nations of Africa. Africa is not a *subject* but merely an *object* of world affairs. Any real change in Africa is inextricably linked to breaking the chains that tie the continent to the existing world order.

INDEX

FORTHCOMING BOOKS
by Kofi Buenor Hadjor

New Perspectives in North-South Dialogue:
Essays in Honour of Olof Palme

This is an edited volume of essays by leading statesmen and thinkers on the North-South dialogue. Contributors include: Samir Amin, Mohamed Babu, Willy Brandt, Gro Harlem Brundtland, Ingvar Carlsson, Fidel Castro, Basil Davidson, Luis Echeverria, Anoushiravan Ehteshami, Andre Gunder Frank, Rajiv Gandhi, Neil Kinnock, Michael Manley, Robert Mugabe, Julius Nyerere, Oliver Tambo and Immanuel Wallerstein.

Osagyefo: Kwame Nkrumah and Africa

Nkrumah and the African liberation movement are inseparable. Nkrumah distilled the experiences and ideologies of the Pan-Africanist movement and came to symbolize that movement when he attained power. This book estimates the relevance of Nkrumah's Pan-African agenda.